Favorite Recipes for

Salads

**By the Editors of Sunset Books
and Sunset Magazine**

Lane Publishing Co. • Menlo Park, California

Salads for All Occasions... from the Classic Waldorf to Exotic Tabbuli

Favorite Recipes for Salads contains just that—
Sunset's choices for the most tempting, time-
honored salad recipes we know of.

You'll find such classics as Caesar, Waldorf,
and Crab Louis; international favorites with exotic
names like Tabbuli and Antipasto; satisfying,
whole-meal salads like Shrimp-stuffed Avocados
and Taco Salad; and meatless, high-protein ones
full of cheese, eggs, sprouts, wheat germ, and
nuts—Protein Health Salad, for example. There
are recipes for refreshing fruit salads and molded
salads, plus more than 75 delicious salad dressings,
including some low-calorie versions.

You'll discover how to make mayonnaise, toast
your own croutons, bottle herb-flavored vinegars,
and unmold gelatin salads. You'll learn about
salad showmanship, and you'll get ideas for
special garnishes and eye-catching containers
which—along with the inventiveness of the
cook—contribute to a salad's success, whether it
introduces a meal, ends a meal, or *is* a meal.

Staff Editors: Judith A. Gaulke
Linda Brandt

Special Consultant: Mary Jane Swanson
Staff Editor, Sunset Magazine

Design: Bud Thon

Photography: Nikolay Zurek
with Lynne B. Morrall

Illustrations: Susan Jaekel, Carol Etow

Cover: Serve-yourself salad (page 9).
Photographed by Nikolay Zurek

Editor, Sunset Books: David E. Clark

First Printing April 1979
Copyright © 1979, 1966, 1962, 1937, Lane Publishing Co.,
Menlo Park, CA 94025. Fourth edition. World rights
Library
of Congress No. 78-70273. ISBN 0-376-02605-7.
Lithographed in the United States.

Honey-cream dressing, page 84, over fresh fruit.

Contents

Special Features

Green & Vegetable Salads

The fresh simplicity of a green salad is the perfect start, finish, or addition to a meal. Equally gifted, the vegetable salad often combines—in crisp, raw form—foods usually served cooked.

Iceberg Salad with Cashews

You pour a hot dressing over this crunchy salad of sunflower seeds, cashews, and bacon bits mixed with crisp iceberg lettuce.

    1   medium-size head iceberg lettuce, broken
            into bite-size pieces
    ⅓   cup thinly sliced green onion
    ½   cup chopped salted cashews
    2   tablespoons chopped parsley
    3   tablespoons roasted sunflower seeds
    3   strips bacon
        Salad oil
    ¼   cup white wine vinegar
    2   teaspoons sugar
        Salt and pepper
    ¼   cup grated Parmesan cheese

In a salad bowl, mix together lettuce, onion, cashews, parsley, and sunflower seeds; set aside.

In a frying pan over medium heat, cook bacon until crisp; drain and crumble into lettuce mixture.

Pour bacon drippings into a measuring cup and add enough salad oil to make ⅓ cup total. Return to pan with vinegar and sugar, and stir until sugar is dissolved. Pour over lettuce and toss well. Season to taste with salt and pepper. Garnish with grated cheese. Makes 6 servings.

Dandelion Greens with Artichoke Hearts

Long, slender dandelion greens have a snappy, slightly bitter flavor. They are available in the produce section of most grocery stores.

    ¾   pound dandelion greens
    3   cups torn romaine leaves
    1   bunch radishes, thinly sliced
    2   jars (6 oz. *each*) marinated artichoke hearts
    2   tablespoons red wine vinegar
    ¼   teaspoon *each* salt and Dijon mustard
    1   clove garlic, minced or pressed

Remove and discard tough stems from dandelion greens. Coarsely chop enough greens to make 3 cups and place in a salad bowl. Mix in romaine and radishes.

Drain marinade from artichoke hearts and combine it with vinegar, salt, mustard, and garlic; blend well. Pour dressing over greens and toss lightly. Arrange artichoke hearts on top. Makes 6 servings.

Crisp Romaine with Bacon Dressing

A last-minute hot bacon dressing is poured over bite-size romaine leaves for an uncomplicated, refreshing meal starter.

About ½ large head romaine, broken into bite-size pieces
⅓ cup thinly sliced green onion
6 strips bacon
2 tablespoons sugar
3 tablespoons wine vinegar
1 egg, well beaten
Salt and pepper

Place romaine and onion in a salad bowl. In a frying pan over medium heat, cook bacon until crisp; drain, crumble, and set aside. Discard all but 3 tablespoons drippings. Stir together sugar, vinegar, and egg; blend into bacon drippings and cook, stirring, over medium-low heat just until hot and slightly thickened.

Remove from heat and season with salt and pepper to taste. Pour over romaine, add bacon, and toss well. Makes about 4 servings.

Romaine with Raisins

Raisins and toasted almonds are tossed with romaine for added flavor and texture. A sweet-tart dressing lends the final touch.

¼ cup salad oil
3 tablespoons catsup
2 tablespoons red wine vinegar
1 tablespoon *each* soy sauce and sugar
½ cup sliced or slivered almonds
1 medium-size avocado
1 large head romaine, broken into bite-size pieces
½ cup golden raisins
6 strips crisply cooked bacon, crumbled
Salt and pepper

Combine oil, catsup, vinegar, soy, and sugar; stir until sugar is dissolved; set aside.

Spread almonds in a shallow pan and toast in a 350° oven until golden (about 8 minutes); set aside.

Peel, pit, and thinly slice avocado. In a salad bowl, mix together romaine, avocado, raisins, almonds, and bacon. Add dressing and toss gently. Season to taste with salt and pepper. Makes 6 to 8 servings.

Iceberg & Green Pea Salad ✓

Bright green frozen peas, quickly thawed, go into this iceberg lettuce salad with sweet onion rings and celery.

Thyme dressing (directions follow)
1 medium-size head iceberg lettuce, broken into bite-size pieces
⅔ cup sliced celery
1 small red onion, thinly sliced
Watercress sprigs (optional)
1 package (10 oz.) frozen peas, thawed
2 or 3 hard-cooked eggs, cut in wedges

Prepare dressing; cover and refrigerate for about 1 hour to allow flavors to blend.

Mix together lettuce, celery, onion, watercress (if desired), and peas. Pour over dressing and toss lightly. Garnish with egg wedges. Makes about 6 servings.

Thyme dressing. Combine ⅓ cup **salad oil,** 2 tablespoons **white wine vinegar,** 1 small clove **garlic** (minced or pressed), 2 teaspoons **Dijon mustard,** ½ teaspoon *each* **thyme leaves** and **sugar,** ¼ teaspoon **pepper,** and 1 teaspoon **salt.**

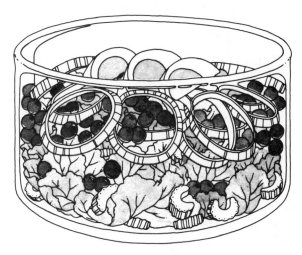

Iceberg & Green Pea Salad (recipe above)

How to Handle Salad Greens

Always handle greens tenderly so they won't bruise. If you have the time, try to wash greens the day before you plan to use them. This gives them time to chill and crisp; then the dressing will coat all leaves thoroughly.

To wash iceberg lettuce, cut out the core, hold the head under running water, and gently separate the leaves just enough to clean them well.

Other types of greens are treated differently. Separate leaves of romaine, butter lettuce, and leaf lettuce and wash each well. For spinach or watercress, open the bunch and wash gently in several changes of water.

Shake off as much water as possible. Discard bruised leaves. Drain the rest well on paper toweling or clean dish towels, or whirl them in a lettuce drying basket.

When greens are well drained and barely damp, wrap them loosely in a clean towel or paper toweling, or place them in large plastic bags. Store in the crisper unit of your refrigerator.

Before serving, pat off any excess moisture and break greens into bite-size pieces; dress and serve.

Greens with Sesame Seed Dressing

This creamy dressing can enhance your choice of salad greens—romaine, butter lettuce, and spinach are good choices.

- ½ cup sesame seed
- 1 cup sour cream
- 2 teaspoons sugar
- 1 teaspoon onion salt
- ⅛ teaspoon pepper
- 1 tablespoon vinegar
- 1 teaspoon Worcestershire
- 1 clove garlic, minced or pressed
- 2½ quarts greens, broken into bite-size pieces (see suggestions above)

In a frying pan over medium-low heat, toast sesame seed, stirring frequently, until browned (about 4 minutes).

Combine sour cream, sugar, onion salt, pepper, vinegar, Worcestershire, garlic, and sesame seed; blend well. Cover and refrigerate, if made ahead.

To serve, pour over greens and toss well. Makes 6 servings.

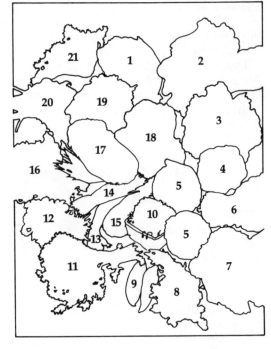

Clockwise: (1.) **ROMAINE** *(cos)—elongated head with long narrow leaves; spicy, mild flavor; juicy and crisp.* (2.) **SWISS CHARD** *(chard)—sturdy, dark green leaves with heavy white stems; leaves good for lining serving bowls.* (3.) **MUSTARD GREENS**—*peppery, bitter, frilly leaves.* (4.) **ICEBERG LETTUCE** *(head)—very crisp, watery; refreshing but mild flavor.* (5.) **HEAD CABBAGE** *(spring head, white, and purple)—tight heads of thick, sturdy leaves, crisp and durable with slight sulfuric taste.* (6.) **SPINACH**—*clean, slightly lemony flavor with dry aftertaste; thick, firm leaves.* (7.) **BUTTER LETTUCE** *(butterhead, Boston. Smaller varieties: bibb or limestone)—very delicate flavor, soft pliable leaves that bruise easily.* (8.) **CORIANDER** *(cilantro, Chinese parsley)—pungent flavor not at all like parsley.* (9.) **BELGIAN ENDIVE** *(French endive, endive)—rich, mildly acrid flavor; waxen, crunchy spears.* (10.) **ALFALFA SPROUTS**—*tiny, crisp, succulent sprouts; grassy flavor.* (11.) **PARSLEY**—*acid sweet; slightly tough leaves.* (12.) **WATERCRESS**—*lively, spicy sweetness to leaves; sharp, biting stalk.* (13.) **GREEN ONIONS**—*sweet with mild piquancy; white end sharper than green.* (14.) **CHIVES**—*dainty, light onion fragrance and flavor.* (15.) **CELERY**—*fibrous, watery, crunchy texture with bland flavor.* (16.) **ESCAROLE** *(broad-leaf endive)—sharp, slightly bitter; rough texture.* (17.) **CHINESE CABBAGE** *(napa, celery cabbage)—mild, delicate, crisp-textured; frilly, pale leaves with celerylike stalks.* (18.) **SAVOY CABBAGE**—*thick, firm leaves on a sturdy, tight cabbage head.* (19.) **RED LEAF LETTUCE** *(leaf)—delicate flavor; tender, fragile leaves with red tips.* (20.) **DANDELION GREENS**—*tart, bitter taste; thin arrow-shaped leaves.* (21.) **CHICORY** *(curly endive)—sprightly, rather bitter flavor; wiry, feathered leaves.*

21) Chicory

(1)
Romaine

(2) Swiss
Chard.

2) Swiss
Chard

3) Mustard
Greens

Curry Dip

1 cup sour cream *or* yogurt
½ tablespoon curry powder
1 tablespoon Tabasco sauce
2 teaspoons instant minced onion
¾ teaspoon salt
1 tablespoon vinegar *or* lemon juice

Combine all ingredients, stirring until thoroughly blended. Serve with carrot and celery sticks, radishes, cucumber slices, scallions, cauliflowerettes or other raw vegetable relishes.

YIELD: About 1 cup.

5

18) Savoy
Cabbage

17) Chinese
Cabbage
(napa or
celery cabbage)

4) iceberg
lettuce

Escarole

14) Chives

15) Celery

6) Spinach

5) Head
Cabbage

13) Green
Onion

12) Water-
cress

10) Alfalfa
Sprouts

5) (also) ✓
Red
Cabbage

11) Parsley

7) Butter
Lettuce

9) BELGIAN
ENDIVE

9) Belgian
Endive

8) Coriander
(cilantro)
or
chinese Parsley

Antipasto Salad

Pictured on page 26

Traditionally served as an Italian appetizer, antipasto ("before the pasta") can become a whole-meal salad. Tempting morsels of vegetables, tuna, anchovies, or sliced salami can be arranged on a bed of greens, then drizzled with an oil-vinegar dressing. Or, lift the salad onto individual plates and pass the dressing. Make as much or as little salad as you have people to serve.

For **greens,** choose romaine, escarole, leaf lettuce, iceberg lettuce, or spinach; add a bit of chicory or dandelion greens for a sharp tang, if you like. You can place the ingredients on whole leaves, or you can break greens into bite-size pieces or shred them to line a basket or serving platter.

Let your imagination, sense of flavor and color, and the ingredients available in your kitchen dictate the assortment you choose for your salad: canned **tuna,** drained; **anchovy fillets,** drained; green or ripe **olives,** whole or sliced; **hard-cooked eggs,** cut in wedges or sliced; **salami,** shredded or cut in pieces; sliced **radishes;** green or red **bell pepper,** sliced or chopped; **parsley; pimento** strips; whole or chopped **green onion; marinated artichoke hearts,** halved or quartered; **marinated mushrooms,** whole or sliced; **Italian pickled vegetables; cherry tomatoes** or medium-size tomatoes, cut in wedges; **green beans,** blanched and chilled; **cauliflowerets,** cut in slices. For a dressing, combine 1 part **red wine vinegar** with 3 parts **olive oil.** Add 1 tablespoon minced **shallots** and ¼ teaspoon **oregano** for each cup dressing.

Egg & Olive Lettuce Salad

Hard-cooked eggs and chopped ripe olives give a distinctive touch to this green salad.

- 1 medium-size head iceberg lettuce, broken into bite-size pieces
- 2 hard-cooked eggs, finely chopped
- 2 tablespoons *each* chopped ripe olives and diced green pepper
- 1 tablespoon finely chopped chives
- ¾ cup salad oil
- ¼ cup wine vinegar or lemon juice
- 1 tablespoon sugar
- 1 teaspoon *each* salt, paprika, and dry mustard
- ¼ teaspoon pepper
  Few drops liquid onion or garlic

In a salad bowl, mix together lettuce, eggs, olives, pepper, and chives.

Combine oil, vinegar, sugar, salt, paprika, mustard, pepper, and liquid onion; blend well. Pour over salad and toss gently. Makes 4 to 6 servings.

Butter Lettuce with Gorgonzola Dressing

This quick-to-make first course adds the zesty flavor of gorgonzola cheese to the basic ingredients of a simple green salad—lettuce with an oil and vinegar dressing.

- ⅔ cup olive oil or salad oil
- ¼ cup lemon juice
- ½ cup coarsely crumbled Gorgonzola cheese
- ½ teaspoon salt
- ¼ teaspoon black pepper
- 6 cups lightly packed butter lettuce leaves, broken into bite-size pieces

Combine oil, lemon juice, cheese, salt, and pepper. Cover and let stand at room temperature for several hours to allow flavors to blend. Chill lettuce until ready to serve.

Shake dressing, pour over lettuce, and toss gently. Makes about 6 servings.

Patio Salad

A refreshing combination of oranges, sweet onions, olives, and a cooling herb dressing is served on a bed of crisp greens and peppery watercress.

- 1 large sweet or mild onion, thinly sliced and separated into rings
- ¼ cup vinegar
- 8 cups bite-size pieces of crisp salad greens
- 2 cups chopped watercress
- 4 oranges
- 1 cup pitted ripe olives, cut in half lengthwise
- 2 tablespoons *each* finely chopped mint and parsley
- ½ cup olive oil or salad oil
- ¼ cup lime juice
- 2 tablespoons honey
- 2 teaspoons crushed dry basil
- ¼ teaspoon paprika
  Dash of cayenne
  Salt

Place onion rings in a small bowl; add vinegar and let stand for about 1 hour, then drain.

Meanwhile, in a large bowl lightly mix salad greens with watercress. Remove peel and white membrane from oranges; lift out sections and arrange on greens along with onion rings and olives. Sprinkle with mint and parsley.

Combine oil, lime juice, honey, basil, paprika, and cayenne; add salt to taste and blend well. Pour over salad and toss gently. Makes 6 to 8 servings.

Overnight Layered Green Salad (recipe below)

Overnight Layered Green Salad

Assemble this salad the night before to allow flavors to mingle. Everything settles on a bed of shredded lettuce, and it makes an impressive presentation when served in a clear glass bowl. You'll need a 3 to 4-quart dish.

- 1 medium-size head iceberg lettuce, shredded
- ½ cup thinly sliced green onion
- 1 cup thinly sliced celery
- 1 can (8 oz.) water chestnuts, drained and sliced
- 1 package (10 oz.) frozen peas
- 2 cups mayonnaise
- 2 teaspoons sugar
- ½ cup grated Parmesan cheese
- 1 teaspoon seasoned salt
- ¼ teaspoon garlic powder
- ½ to ¾ pound bacon, crisply cooked
- 3 hard-cooked eggs, chopped
- 2 medium-size tomatoes, cut into wedges

Serve-yourself Salad Bar... For a Light, Informal Entrée

Pictured on front cover

Next time you plan a casual lunch or a light, informal dinner, why not let a salad bar do main-dish duty? A serve-yourself salad bar has real advantages—it guarantees to please individual tastes, and, because most of the preparation can be done in advance, it frees the host and hostess to enjoy the meal as much as the guests do.

Included at the salad bar should be a large bowl of torn, crisp greens and a choice of three or four different dressings. The remaining ingredients—meat, cheese, eggs, and vegetables—can be attractively arranged on a large tray or in a shallow lettuce-lined bowl (see cover photograph). Or you may prefer to present each ingredient in its own bowl to serve buffet-style or pass at the table.

For *each* serving allow about **2½ to 3 cups crisp salad greens** such as romaine, butter or iceberg lettuce, or spinach, torn into bitesize pieces; **3 to 4 ounces cold cooked meat** such as ham or turkey, cut into strips; **2 ounces Cheddar or Swiss cheese,** cut into strips; and **½ to 1 hard-cooked egg,** cut in half.

Offer, too, a variety of garnishes such as whole **cherry tomatoes** and pitted **ripe olives,** sliced **carrots** and **avocados, alfalfa sprouts, marinated artichoke hearts,** quartered or sliced **mushrooms,** pickled or waterpacked **baby corn,** and roasted **Spanish peanuts.**

A good choice of **dressings** would include an all-purpose vinaigrette (recipe on page 87), a mustard-tarragon dressing (recipe on page 88), a creamy blue cheese (recipe on page 89), and a green goddess dressing (recipes on page 90).

In a 3 to 4-quart shallow glass serving bowl, make a layer of shredded lettuce. Top with a layer *each* of onion, celery, water chestnuts, and frozen peas. Spread evenly with mayonnaise. Sprinkle with sugar, cheese, salt, and garlic powder. Cover and refrigerate for several hours or until next day.

Crumble bacon into salad. Sprinkle with chopped eggs. Arrange tomato wedges around salad.

To serve, use a spoon and fork to lift out each serving, which should include some of each layer. Makes 8 to 10 servings.

Caesar Salad

Pictured on facing page

At the last minute, crack a fresh egg over romaine leaves coated with garlic-flavored oil. Add lemon juice for tartness; Parmesan cheese and anchovies round out the traditional touches.

> 1 small clove garlic, minced or pressed
> ⅓ cup olive oil or salad oil
> 1 cup croutons, purchased or homemade (see page 69)
> 1 large head romaine, broken into bite-size pieces
> Salt and pepper
> 1 egg
> Boiling water
> About 2 tablespoons lemon juice
> 3 to 4 anchovy fillets, drained and chopped
> ¼ cup grated Parmesan cheese

If time permits, combine garlic and oil and let stand for several hours. In a frying pan over medium heat, brown croutons in 2 tablespoons of the garlic-flavored oil, stirring frequently; set aside.

Place romaine in a salad bowl; sprinkle with salt and pepper to taste. Pour remaining garlic oil over romaine and toss until leaves are thoroughly coated.

Slip egg into boiling water for 1 minute; remove and break into salad. Drizzle lemon juice over all and mix thoroughly. Add anchovies and grated cheese; mix thoroughly. Add croutons and toss. Makes 6 servings.

Sprout-Spinach Salad

Garnish this spinach and bean sprout salad with sliced hard-cooked eggs. You can prepare the salad and dressing ahead, if you like, then mix them together just before serving.

> 1 large bunch spinach
> ½ pound fresh bean sprouts
> 1 can (6 oz.) water chestnuts, drained and sliced
> 5 strips crisply cooked bacon, crumbled
> ⅔ cup salad oil
> ⅓ cup *each* sugar, catsup, red wine vinegar, and finely chopped onion
> 2 teaspoons Worcestershire
> Salt and pepper
> 2 hard-cooked eggs, sliced

UNCOMPLICATED CAESAR SALAD is a traditional romaine lettuce salad simply dressed with lemon, anchovy, egg, and a last-minute grating of Parmesan cheese. The recipe is on this page.

Remove and discard tough spinach stems. Break leaves into bite-size pieces. In a salad bowl, mix together spinach, bean sprouts, water chestnuts, and bacon. Cover and refrigerate, if made ahead.

Combine oil, sugar, catsup, vinegar, onion, and Worcestershire; blend well. Pour over spinach and toss gently until well mixed; season to taste with salt and pepper. Garnish with sliced eggs. Makes 8 servings.

Greek Spinach Salad

Look for the canned grape leaves in the gourmet section of your market, and the slightly salty feta cheese with other imported cheeses in the refrigerated section. These added touches give this whole-meal salad a distinctly Greek flavor.

> 1 jar (6 oz.) marinated artichoke hearts
> 1 tablespoon olive oil or salad oil
> 2 tablespoons lemon juice
> ½ teaspoon *each* dry basil leaves and dry mustard
> Dash of pepper
> 1 large bunch spinach
> 3 green onions, thinly sliced
> 1 small cucumber, sliced (optional)
> 1 hard-cooked egg, sliced
> 5 or 6 cherry tomatoes, halved
> ½ can (13-oz. size) rice-stuffed grape leaves, drained (optional)
> ⅛ pound mushrooms, sliced
> About 3 ounces feta cheese, crumbled
> Dried cured olives or sliced ripe olives

Into a small bowl, drain marinade from artichoke hearts (reserve hearts). To marinade, add oil, lemon juice, basil, mustard, and pepper; blend well and set aside.

Remove and discard tough spinach stems; break leaves into bite-size pieces. Place in a salad bowl, add onion and cucumber, and mix. Arrange in rows on top of spinach: egg, artichoke hearts, cherry tomatoes, grape leaves, and mushrooms; sprinkle on feta cheese and olives.

At the table, pour on dressing and mix gently. Makes 4 to 6 servings.

Spinach Salad with Bacon & Apples

Tart apples, toasted almonds, and crumbled bacon bits transform an ordinary spinach salad into something special.

(Continued on next page)

2 **large bunches spinach**
6 **strips bacon**
⅓ **cup sliced almonds**
¼ **cup olive oil or salad oil**
3 **tablespoons tarragon wine vinegar
   or white wine vinegar**
⅛ **teaspoon salt**
1 **teaspoon sugar**
½ **teaspoon dry mustard**
   Dash pepper
1 **large red-skinned apple**
3 **tablespoons sliced green onion**

Remove and discard tough spinach stems; wash leaves, drain well, and chill for at least 2 hours.

Meanwhile, in a frying pan over medium heat, cook bacon until crisp; drain (reserving 1 tablespoon drippings), crumble, and set aside. Place almonds in remaining bacon drippings and sauté until lightly browned (about 3 or 4 minutes); lift from pan and set aside.

Combine oil, vinegar, salt, sugar, mustard, and pepper; blend well. Core and dice apple. Break spinach into bite-size pieces and place in a large bowl; add onion, apple, and almonds. Pour dressing over salad and toss gently. Makes 6 to 8 servings.

Spinach-Cauliflower Toss

Pictured on page 23

Because this salad doesn't wilt readily, it's a good one to serve with a buffet dinner. Garnish the contrasting green and white salad with avocado slices.

½ **cup pine nuts or slivered almonds**
½ **large bunch spinach, torn into bite-size pieces**
  **About ½ medium-size head cauliflower,
   broken into flowerets, then cut in
   ¼-inch-thick slices**
1 **large avocado**
  Lemon juice
6 **tablespoons salad oil**
3 **tablespoons white wine vinegar**
1 **large clove garlic, minced or pressed**
½ **teaspoon *each* salt, dry mustard,
   and dry basil leaves**
¼ **teaspoon pepper**
  Dash of ground nutmeg

Spread nuts in a shallow pan and toast in a 350° oven until lightly browned (about 8 minutes). Set aside. Place spinach and cauliflower in a bowl. Peel, pit, and slice avocado. Dip avocado slices in lemon juice to coat. Add to vegetables.

Combine oil, vinegar, garlic, salt, mustard, basil, pepper, and nutmeg; blend well. Pour over vegetables; add nuts and gently mix to coat thoroughly. Makes 6 servings.

Swiss Chard with Lemon-Oil Dressing

From the Middle East comes this unusual way to serve greens as a salad.

1 **large bunch (about 1 lb.) Swiss chard
  Boiling water**
1 **teaspoon salt**
¼ **cup olive oil or salad oil**
1½ **tablespoons lemon juice**
¼ **teaspoon Dijon mustard (optional)
  Chopped chives or parsley (optional)**

Wash chard leaves well; trim off and discard stem ends. Cut out the heavy white part (remaining stem) of each leaf and slice crosswise into ½-inch-wide pieces. Then slice leaves crosswise into ½-inch-wide pieces; keep green and white parts separate.

Place stems in about ½ inch of boiling water with salt. Cover and cook for 3 to 4 minutes; add leaves, cover, and continue cooking for 3 to 4 more minutes or until tender to bite. Drain, pressing out excess water.

Combine oil, lemon juice, and mustard (if used). Turn chard into a salad bowl, add dressing, and toss gently. Garnish with chives, if desired. Makes 4 servings.

Easy Coleslaw

Here's a tasty, all-purpose coleslaw that goes together in minutes.

1 **cup mayonnaise**
4 **tablespoons Dijon mustard**
2 **tablespoons dill pickle liquid**
⅔ **cup sliced green onion**
8 **cups finely shredded cabbage**

Combine mayonnaise, mustard, pickle liquid, and onion. Place cabbage in a large salad bowl, add mayonnaise mixture, and toss gently until thoroughly mixed. Cover and refrigerate for at least 1 hour or until next day. Makes 8 to 10 servings.

Oriental Cabbage Slaw

Curly-leaved Chinese cabbage, edible-pod peas, and bamboo shoots give this salad an Oriental touch, and the sweet soy dressing punctuates the message.

- ½ pound fresh edible-pod peas, ends and strings removed, or 1 package (10 oz.) frozen edible-pod peas, thawed
- 1 small head (about 1¼ lbs.) Chinese cabbage (napa), coarsely shredded
- 1 medium-size bunch radishes, thinly sliced
- ½ cup thinly sliced green onion
- 1 can (8½ oz.) sliced bamboo shoots, drained
- ⅔ cup slivered almonds
  Sweet soy dressing (directions follow)

Cut pea pods into 1-inch pieces. Place in a salad bowl with cabbage, radishes, onion, and bamboo shoots; cover and refrigerate, if made ahead.

Spread almonds in a shallow pan and toast in a 350° oven until lightly browned (about 8 minutes); set aside.

Prepare dressing, add to cabbage mixture, and toss well. Garnish with toasted almonds. Makes 6 to 8 servings.

Sweet soy dressing. Combine ½ cup **salad oil**, ⅓ cup **white wine vinegar**, 3 tablespoons **sugar**, 2 tablespoons **soy sauce**, ¾ teaspoon **ground ginger**, ⅛ teaspoon **cayenne**, and ¼ teaspoon **sesame oil** (optional); blend well.

Red Cabbage Slaw

A colorful combination salad of red cabbage, green pepper, parsley, and celery is topped with a creamy mayonnaise dressing.

- 8 cups finely shredded red cabbage
- 1 medium-size green pepper, cut in thin strips
- ¼ cup finely chopped parsley
- ½ cup chopped dill pickle
- ½ cup *each* sliced celery and green onion (including part of the green tops)
  Sour cream cabbage dressing (directions follow)

In a large bowl, combine cabbage, pepper, parsley, pickle, celery, and onion. Cover and refrigerate for at least 1 hour.

Just before serving, prepare sour cream cabbage dressing. Pour over cabbage mixture, toss gently, and serve. Makes 6 to 8 servings.

Sour cream cabbage dressing. Combine ⅔ cup **sour cream** with ⅓ cup **mayonnaise**. Add 1 teaspoon *each* **Dijon mustard, salt, sugar,** and **celery**

seed; ¼ teaspoon **pepper**; and 2 tablespoons **wine vinegar**. Mix until well blended.

Bean Sprout-Vegetable Slaw

It's fun to vary your coleslaw with a combination of cabbages. You might want to try Chinese (napa) with red cabbage or the familiar spring head cabbage. Then add crisp vegetables and Spanish peanuts for that extra crunch.

- 5 cups finely shredded cabbage
- ½ cup sliced green onion or chopped red onion
- 1 small red or green bell pepper, diced
- 1 cup thinly sliced celery or carrot
- ¼ pound bean sprouts
- 1 can (6 oz.) water chestnuts, drained and thinly sliced
  Sweet pickle dressing (directions follow)
- ½ cup dry roasted Spanish-style peanuts

In a salad bowl, mix together cabbage, onion, pepper, celery, sprouts, and water chestnuts. Prepare dressing, pour over cabbage mixture, and toss gently. Garnish with peanuts. Makes 4 to 6 servings.

Sweet pickle dressing. Combine 1 cup **mayonnaise**, 1 tablespoon **mustard seed**, 1½ teaspoons *each* **prepared horseradish** and **Worcestershire**, 2 tablespoons **sweet pickle relish**, and ¼ teaspoon **salt**.

Peas & Peanut Slaw

Sour cream and a touch of curry add flavor to this coleslaw. Sprinkle Spanish-style peanuts over it just before serving to add extra protein and texture.

- 1 package (10 oz.) frozen peas, thawed
- 2 cups finely shredded cabbage
- 1 green onion, thinly sliced
- ¼ cup *each* sour cream and mayonnaise
- ¼ teaspoon *each* salt and curry powder
  Dash of pepper
- 1 teaspoon *each* prepared mustard and wine vinegar
- ¾ cup salted Spanish-style peanuts

In a salad bowl, mix together peas, cabbage, and onion. In a small bowl, combine sour cream, mayonnaise, salt, curry powder, pepper, mustard, and vinegar; blend well. Pour over cabbage mixture and toss lightly. Cover and refrigerate for at least 1 hour or until next day.

Garnish with peanuts before serving. Makes 4 to 6 servings.

Crunchy Pea Salad

Vegetables chill in a soy marinade before being mixed with mayonnaise to spoon over lettuce leaves. Everything gets a sprinkling of crumbled bacon.

- 1 package (10 oz.) frozen peas, thawed
- 1 can (6 oz.) water chestnuts, drained and sliced
- 3 or 4 stalks celery, thinly sliced
- 1 cup coarsely shredded carrot
- 3 or 4 green onions, thinly sliced
  Soy marinade (directions follow)
- 4 tablespoons mayonnaise
  Salt and pepper
  Lettuce leaves
- 4 strips crisply cooked bacon, crumbled

In a salad bowl, mix together peas, water chestnuts, celery, carrot, and onion. Prepare marinade and pour over salad; mix well. Cover and refrigerate for 30 minutes or as long as 3 hours.

To serve, drain off and discard marinade from salad. Add mayonnaise to salad, then salt and pepper to taste; mix well. Arrange lettuce on 4 individual salad plates or in a salad bowl. Spoon equal amounts of salad on lettuce. Garnish with crumbled bacon. Makes 4 servings.

Soy marinade. Combine 2 tablespoons *each* **salad oil** and **wine vinegar;** 1 tablespoon **soy sauce;** 1 teaspoon *each* **sugar, paprika,** and **dry mustard;** 1/2 teaspoon **salt;** and 1 small clove **garlic** (minced or pressed).

Swiss Green Pea Salad

Swiss cheese, bacon, and peas make this salad substantial enough for a light meal.

- 1/2 cup mayonnaise
- 1 teaspoon sugar
- 1/2 teaspoon ground nutmeg
- 1 1/2 teaspoons Dijon mustard
- 2 quarts torn romaine or iceberg lettuce leaves
- 6 strips crisply cooked bacon, crumbled
- 6 ounces Swiss cheese, cut into matchstick-size pieces
- 1 package (10 oz.) frozen peas, thawed
- 1 small red onion, thinly sliced
- 2 stalks celery, thinly sliced
  Salt and pepper

Combine mayonnaise, sugar, nutmeg, and mustard; set aside. In a salad bowl, mix together lettuce, bacon (reserve 2 tablespoons), cheese, peas, onion, and celery. Pour over dressing and toss

gently to coat evenly. Season to taste with salt and pepper. Garnish with reserved bacon. Makes 4 to 6 servings.

Green Bean-Garbanzo Salad with Basil

A two-bean salad, made from frozen and canned beans, marinates for a few hours in basil dressing.

- 2 packages (10 oz. *each*) frozen French-cut green beans, thawed
- 1 cup (about 15 oz.) garbanzos, drained
- 1 cup thinly sliced celery
- 1 clove garlic, minced or pressed
- 1/4 cup *each* wine vinegar and salad oil
- 1 tablespoon sugar
- 1/2 teaspoon *each* salt and dry basil

In a salad bowl, mix together green beans, garbanzos, celery, and garlic. Combine vinegar, oil, sugar, salt, and basil; blend well and pour over beans. Toss gently until vegetables are well coated; cover and refrigerate for at least 2 hours or until next day.

To serve, toss salad gently. Makes 6 to 8 servings.

Baby Lima Salad

Green onion, shredded carrot, bacon, and eggs give color and crunch to a tender lima bean salad. This is a salad that can chill overnight and be all ready for the next day.

- 1 package (10 oz.) frozen baby lima beans
- 5 strips bacon
- 1/2 cup *each* sliced celery and thinly sliced green onion
- 1/3 cup shredded carrot
- 1 jar (2 oz.) sliced pimento, drained
- 2 hard-cooked eggs, chopped
- 1/3 cup mayonnaise
- 2 teaspoons prepared mustard
- 1 tablespoon lemon juice
  Salt and pepper

Cook limas according to package directions until tender. Drain, plunge into cold water, and drain again.

In a wide frying pan over medium heat, cook bacon until crisp. Drain, crumble, set aside 1 tablespoon, and add remaining bacon to limas. Stir in

(Continued on page 19)

FOR ELEGANCE, serve these individual first-course salads of slender asparagus spears garnished with marinated artichoke hearts, watercress sprigs, and a sprinkling of chopped pimento. The recipe is on page 16.

When serving a more elegant meal with several courses, you can begin or end with individual salads—to stimulate the appetite or clear the palate. Here are a number of first-course salads incorporating make-ahead steps in their preparation. Greens can be washed and chilled a day in advance. Many use canned ingredients for easy availability. All can be served attractively with little effort.

Artichokes with Watercress Salad

Lacy watercress and garlic-seasoned canned artichoke hearts make a handsome, zestful salad.

- 2 cans (14 oz. *each*) water-packed artichoke hearts, drained
- 2 tablespoons wine vinegar
- 4 tablespoons olive oil or salad oil
- ½ teaspoon garlic salt
- 3 cups lightly packed watercress leaves (about 2 bunches)

Combine artichokes with vinegar, oil, and garlic salt; cover and let stand at room temperature for 1 to 6 hours.

Distribute watercress leaves equally among 6 individual salad plates. Spoon an equal number of artichoke hearts onto each plate; drizzle evenly with marinade. Makes 6 servings.

Spinach Salad with Pine Nut Dressing

Golden, faintly resinous pine nuts season this first-course spinach salad.

- ⅔ cup pine nuts
- 7 tablespoons olive oil or salad oil
- 2½ tablespoons wine vinegar
- ⅛ teaspoon ground nutmeg
- ½ teaspoon *each* grated lemon peel, tarragon leaves, and salt
- 1½ bunches (about 1¾ lbs.) spinach

Spread pine nuts in a single layer in a shallow pan. Toast in a 350° oven, stirring occasionally, until golden (5 to 8 minutes). Let cool, then blend with oil, vinegar, nutmeg, lemon peel, tarragon, and salt. Cover and let stand at room temperature for at least 30 minutes or until next day.

Select large spinach leaves to line each of 8 individual salad plates. Thinly sliver remaining spinach and mound onto plates. Stir pine nut dressing to blend, then spoon an equal portion over each salad. Makes 8 servings.

Hearts of Palm & Shrimp Salad

Romaine spears are the sturdy background for this delicate pink, white, and green combination.

- 1 can (14 oz.) hearts of palm, drained
- 2 tablespoons white wine vinegar
- 4 tablespoons olive oil or salad oil
- 3 tablespoons minced green onion
- ⅓ pound small cooked shrimp
  Salt
  Romaine leaves

Cut each heart of palm stalk crosswise into ½-inch-thick slices; place in deep bowl. Combine vinegar, oil, green onion, shrimp, and salt to taste; mix gently with hearts of palm. Cover and chill 2 to 6 hours.

Arrange several romaine leaves on each of 6 individual salad plates. Spoon equal portions of the hearts of palm mixture onto romaine. Makes 6 servings.

Asparagus & Marinated Artichoke Salad

Pictured on page 15

Marinated artichokes and asparagus go together quickly for this luxurious salad.

- 2 jars (6 oz. *each*) marinated artichoke hearts
- 2 tablespoons minced green onion
- 2 cans (about 15 oz. *each*) green or green-tipped white asparagus spears, drained
  Watercress or parsley
  Chopped pimento

Combine artichoke hearts and their marinade with onion. (At this point you can let stand, covered, for as long as 4 hours at room temperature.)

Distribute asparagus spears equally among 6 individual salad plates. Spoon an equal portion of artichokes over each portion and moisten with marinade. Garnish with watercress and pimento. Makes 6 servings.

Leeks Vinaigrette

Leeks, the mild-flavored members of the onion family that look like giant green onions, blend well with simple seasonings. Wash them well, as dirt hides in their nooks and crannies.

    2 pounds leeks
      Boiling water
 ½ cup olive oil
    1 teaspoon *each* chives and instant
        minced onion
 ¼ teaspoon *each* tarragon leaves
        and salt
      Dash pepper
    1 hard-cooked egg
    1 tablespoon chopped parsley
      Lemon wedges

Cut off root ends of leeks and trim tops so leeks are about 7 inches long. Split in half lengthwise to within ¾ inch of bulb end. Strip away outer layers of leaves to reach nonfibrous leaves inside. Hold under running water, separating leaves to wash.

In a large frying pan over high heat, immerse leeks in 1 inch boiling water and cook, covered, until tender when pierced (about 10 minutes); drain.

Combine oil, chives, onion, tarragon, salt, and pepper. Pour over leeks; cover and chill for about 1 hour.

Meanwhile, press egg through a wire strainer; blend with parsley.

To serve, remove leeks from dressing with a slotted spoon and place on a serving platter. Spoon over 2 tablespoons of the dressing; top with egg mixture. Pass lemon wedges to squeeze over. Makes 4 to 6 servings.

Limestone Salad with Shallot Dressing

A little limestone lettuce goes a long way when paired with red leaf or tender butter lettuce. Limestone lettuce is sometimes hard to find. If unavailable, substitute hearts of butter lettuce.

      Red leaf or butter lettuce leaves
 ½ pound limestone lettuce or 2 small
        heads butter lettuce
    2 tablespoons wine vinegar
    1 teaspoon Dijon mustard
    2 tablespoons minced shallots
 ¼ teaspoon salt
    7 tablespoons olive oil or salad oil

Arrange 3 or 4 red leaf lettuce leaves on each of 6 individual salad plates. Separate limestone lettuce into individual leaves and distribute evenly on red lettuce.

Combine vinegar, mustard, shallots, salt, and oil; blend well. Spoon dressing equally over each salad. Makes 6 servings.

Avocado-Papaya Salad

Papaya wedges topped with chunks of avocado and segments of fresh oranges make a pretty start for a special meal.

    6 tablespoons lime juice
    1 tablespoon honey
 ¼ teaspoon bitters
    2 medium-size avocados
    3 medium-size oranges
    2 large papayas, peeled, halved, pitted,
        then cut in quarters lengthwise

Combine lime juice, honey, and bitters. Peel and pit avocados; cut in large chunks. Add avocado, turning to coat. Remove peel and white membrane from oranges; lift out sections.

Arrange 1 papaya section on each of 6 salad plates; top evenly with avocado mixture and orange slices. Makes 6 servings.

Endive Salad with Curry Dressing

Pale Belgian endive tops butter lettuce in this dramatic-looking salad.

    2 tablespoons wine vinegar
    5 tablespoons olive oil or salad oil
 ½ teaspoon *each* Worcestershire and
        Dijon mustard
 ¼ teaspoon *each* curry powder and salt
 ⅛ teaspoon *each* ground cardamom
        and cayenne
    2 large heads butter lettuce
 ½ pound Belgian endive
    1 large lemon, cut into 6 thin slices

Combine vinegar, oil, Worcestershire, mustard, curry, salt, cardamom, and cayenne. (If made ahead, keep at room temperature.)

Arrange 3 or 4 butter lettuce leaves on each of 6 individual salad plates. Separate endive into leaves and arrange decoratively on lettuce, dividing equally among plates. Top each salad with lemon slice, then drizzle with equal amounts of dressing. Makes 6 servings.

...*Baby Lima Salad (cont'd.)*

celery, onion, carrot, and pimento. Set aside 1 tablespoon egg; add remaining egg to lima mixture.

In a small bowl, combine mayonnaise, mustard, and lemon juice; stir into lima mixture. Add salt and pepper to taste, cover, and refrigerate for several hours or until next day. To serve, stir well and top with reserved bacon and egg. Makes 4 to 6 servings.

Celery Heart Salad

Keep this cool salad in mind when you plan to have a spicy entrée. You spoon dressing over the lightly cooked celery topped with egg slices, then add a squeeze of lemon.

    3 celery hearts, *each* about 2 inches in
           diameter
       Boiling water
    ½ cup sour cream or unflavored yogurt
    ½ cup tomato-based chili sauce
    1½ teaspoons Worcestershire
    1 teaspoon prepared horseradish
    ⅛ teaspoon liquid hot pepper seasoning
       Salt and pepper
       Lettuce leaves
    3 tablespoons chopped green onion
    2 hard-cooked eggs, shelled and sliced
    6 lemon wedges

Trim celery hearts so each is about 6 inches long; reserve trimmings for other uses. Split each celery heart in half lengthwise.

Bring about 1 inch water to boil in a wide frying pan. Add celery; cover and simmer for 6 to 8 minutes or just until tender when pierced. Drain, plunge into cold water, then drain again. Cover and chill for several hours or until next day.

Mix together sour cream, chili sauce, Worcestershire, horseradish, hot pepper seasoning, and salt and pepper to taste; cover and chill.

To serve, place celery hearts on 6 individual lettuce-lined plates; garnish evenly with onion, egg slices, and lemon wedges. Pass dressing to spoon over. Makes 6 servings.

Baked Bean Salad

Canned pork and beans and crunchy raw vegetables make a hearty salad. If you plan to carry this salad to a picnic, omit the lettuce and garnish with sliced hard-cooked eggs.

GARDEN-FRESH AND GOOD FOR YOU,
this high-protein vegetable salad is chock-full of grains, sprouts, nuts, cheese, and vegetables. The recipe is on this page.

    ¼ cup light molasses
    1 tablespoon prepared mustard
    2 tablespoons *each* salad oil and cider
           vinegar
    1 large can (1 lb. 15 oz.) pork and beans
           with tomato sauce
    1 cup *each* diced cooked ham and thinly
           sliced celery
    ½ cup *each* sliced green onion, chopped
           carrot, chopped sweet pickle, and diced
           sharp Cheddar cheese
    1 large tomato, peeled and diced
       Salt and pepper
    3 cups shredded iceberg lettuce or
           2 to 3 sliced hard-cooked eggs

In a large bowl, combine molasses, mustard, oil, and vinegar; blend well. Discard pork fat from beans; add beans and their sauce to vinegar mixture along with ham, celery, onion, carrot, pickle, cheese, and tomato. Mix gently until well coated. Cover and chill for at least 2 hours or until next day.

To serve, arrange shredded lettuce in a shallow salad bowl. Stir bean mixture, then spoon over lettuce. (Or omit lettuce and garnish with egg slices.) Makes 6 to 8 servings.

Protein Health Salad

Pictured on facing page

Meatless as it is, this nutritious green salad is full of protein derived from peanuts, wheat germ, cheese, and eggs.

    2 large butter lettuce heads
    8 to 10 medium-size mushrooms
    1 carrot, sliced
    ½ cup Spanish-style peanuts
    3 tablespoons chopped parsley
    2 tablespoons *each* toasted wheat germ and
           sunflower seeds
    2 tablespoons granola-type cereal
    ½ cup *each* bean sprouts and shredded jack
           cheese
    ¾ cup unflavored yogurt
    3 tablespoons salad oil
    1½ tablespoons lemon juice
       Salt and pepper
    1 small avocado
    2 hard-cooked eggs, quartered

Line a large serving bowl with outer lettuce leaves. Break remaining leaves into bite-size pieces. Place in bowl and mix with mushrooms, carrot, and peanuts. Sprinkle in parsley, wheat germ, sunflower seeds, cereal, sprouts, and cheese. Combine yogurt, oil, and lemon juice; blend well. Pour dressing over salad; toss gently. Season to taste with salt and pepper. Peel, pit, and slice avocado. Garnish with eggs and avocado slices. Makes 4 to 6 servings.

Picnic Potato Salad

Like many potato salads, this version tastes even better if made well in advance and allowed to chill thoroughly.

    6 medium-size potatoes (about 2½ lbs. total)
      Boiling water
   12 green onions, including part of the
        green tops, sliced
    4 hard-cooked eggs, chopped
    1 cup thinly sliced celery
   12 strips crisply cooked bacon, crumbled
    1 jar (4 oz.) sliced pimentos, drained
    1 cup chopped dill pickle
   1½ cups mayonnaise
    1 tablespoon prepared horseradish
    2 teaspoons prepared mustard
    1 tablespoon dill pickle liquid (optional)
      Salt and pepper

Place potatoes in 1 inch of boiling water; cover and cook until tender when pierced (about 25 minutes). Drain, cool, peel, and cut into cubes.

Place potatoes in a large salad bowl. Add onion slices (reserve some of the green tops for garnish), eggs, celery, bacon, pimentos, and pickle. Combine mayonnaise, horseradish, mustard, and pickle liquid (if used); blend well. Stir into potato mixture; season to taste with salt and pepper and garnish with reserved onion tops. Cover and chill for 4 to 6 hours or until next day. Makes 12 to 14 servings.

New Potato Salad with Caviar

For an elegant dinner buffet salad, serve thinly sliced new potatoes sprinkled with lumpfish caviar. It's a make-ahead idea that will get raves and recipe requests.

   2½ pounds thin-skinned new potatoes
      Boiling salted water
   ⅔ cup salad oil
   ⅓ cup white wine vinegar
   ½ teaspoon *each* dry mustard and sugar
    1 teaspoon salt
   ¼ teaspoon pepper
   ½ teaspoon dill weed
   ½ cup chopped green onion
    1 jar (about 4 oz.) lumpfish caviar
      Parsley sprigs

Place potatoes in 1 inch boiling water; cover and cook just until tender when pierced (about 30 minutes). Drain and cool (peel, if desired); then cut into ¼-inch-thick slices. Arrange potatoes in a shallow dish.

In a bowl, combine oil, vinegar, mustard, sugar, salt, and pepper; blend well. Stir in dill weed and ¼ cup of the onion. Pour over potatoes, cover, and refrigerate for at least 4 hours or until next day.

Spoon caviar into a strainer and rinse with cool water; let drain for several minutes. Arrange potato slices slightly overlapping in rows on platter. Spoon remaining dressing from bottom of dish over potatoes; sprinkle with caviar and remaining onion. Garnish with parsley sprigs. Makes 8 servings.

French-style Potato Salad

Colorful, waxy-textured round red potatoes are best for this piquant salad. The tart, peppery seasoning distinguishes it from standard potato salads.

    4 large red new potatoes
        (about 2½ lbs. total)
      Boiling water
   ⅓ cup finely chopped parsley
    1 small onion, finely chopped
    1 tablespoon Dijon mustard
    1 teaspoon salt
   ¼ teaspoon pepper
   ¾ teaspoon tarragon leaves
    1 or 2 cloves garlic, minced or pressed
   ½ cup white wine vinegar
   ⅔ cup olive oil or salad oil

Place potatoes in 1 inch of boiling water; cover and cook until tender when pierced (about 30 minutes). Drain, let stand for about 10 minutes, and cut into ⅜-inch slices.

Place potatoes in a large salad bowl. Add parsley and onion. Blend together mustard, salt, pepper, tarragon, garlic, vinegar, and oil. Pour over potato mixture and toss gently to coat. Cover and let stand at room temperature for at least 3 hours; chill, if desired. Makes 8 servings.

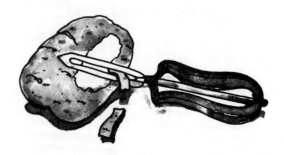

German Potato Salad

Bologna, apples, and anchovies make this version of sweet-tart German potato salad an agreeable change from the standard picnic variety. It can be served warm or cold.

    4 large thin-skinned potatoes
       (about 1½ lbs. total)
       Boiling water
    1 large red onion, finely chopped
    6 slices bologna, diced
    1 red apple, diced
    1 stalk celery, thinly sliced
    1 can (2 oz.) anchovy fillets, drained and
       chopped
    2 tablespoons grated Parmesan cheese
    4 strips bacon
    ¼ cup vinegar
    2 teaspoons sugar
    ½ teaspoon *each* salt and Worcestershire
    ¼ teaspoon garlic salt
    ⅛ teaspoon pepper
    1 egg yolk

Place potatoes in 1 inch boiling water; cover and cook just until tender when pierced (about 30 minutes); drain and cool. In a salad bowl, mix together onion, bologna, apple, celery, anchovies, and Parmesan cheese. Dice potatoes (peel, if desired) and add to bologna mixture.

In a frying pan over medium heat, cook bacon until crisp; drain and crumble into salad. Discard all but 3 tablespoons drippings. Stir together vinegar, sugar, salt, Worcestershire, garlic salt, pepper, and egg yolk; blend into bacon drippings and cook, stirring, over low heat just until hot and slightly thickened. Pour over potato mixture, mix gently but thoroughly, and serve warm. Makes about 8 servings.

Curried Peanut Potato Salad

Salted peanuts and peanut butter are the surprising ingredients in this potato salad variation. Make it at least 4 hours ahead to allow flavors to blend.

    2 pounds thin-skinned potatoes
       Boiling water
    ½ cup *each* chopped green pepper and celery
    ¾ cup thinly sliced green onion
    ¼ cup *each* lightly packed chopped parsley
       and diced cucumber
    6 strips crisply cooked bacon, crumbled
    ¾ cup salted Spanish-style peanuts
    ½ cup mayonnaise
    2 tablespoons cider vinegar
    1 tablespoon chunk-style peanut butter
    1 teaspoon curry powder
       Salt and pepper

Place potatoes in 1 inch boiling water; cover and cook just until tender when pierced (about 30 minutes); drain. When cool, peel (if desired) and cut into ½-inch cubes.

In a salad bowl, mix together potatoes, green pepper, celery, onion, parsley, cucumber, bacon, and ½ cup of the nuts.

Combine mayonnaise, vinegar, peanut butter, and curry; blend well. Add to potato mixture; mix thoroughly but gently. Season to taste with salt and pepper. Cover and refrigerate for at least 4 hours or until next day. Just before serving, stir well and garnish with remaining nuts. Makes 6 servings.

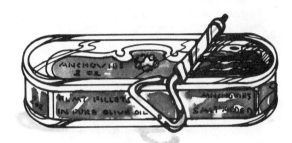

Parsley-Anchovy Potato Salad

This variation of old-fashioned potato salad is punctuated with green—from parsley, green onion, and celery. It's a favorite of the picnic crowd.

    2 pounds white thin-skinned potatoes
       Boiling water
    ½ cup *each* finely chopped parsley and celery
    ⅓ cup finely chopped green onion
    1 hard-cooked egg
    1 small clove garlic, minced or pressed
    4 canned anchovy fillets
    2 tablespoons Dijon mustard
    ½ teaspoon sugar
    ¼ teaspoon liquid hot pepper seasoning
    6 tablespoons olive oil or salad oil
    3 tablespoons white wine vinegar
       Salt and pepper

Place potatoes in 1 inch boiling water; cover and cook just until tender when pierced (about 30 minutes). Drain, cool, peel (if desired), and thinly slice into a salad bowl. Add parsley, celery, and onion.

In a small bowl, mash together egg, garlic, and anchovies. Blend in mustard, sugar, hot pepper seasoning, oil, and vinegar. Pour over potatoes and mix gently. Season to taste with salt and pepper. Cool, cover, and refrigerate for at least 4 hours or until next day. Makes 6 to 8 servings.

Greenst Veg. Salade (cont.) chpt. 1

Spring Vegetable Salade Niçoise

A bounty of spring vegetables makes this version of the popular French Niçoise salad colorful and hearty. Anchovies and Dijon mustard flavor the dressing. Use the extra anchovies to garnish the salad, if you like.

- ¾ pound small thin-skinned potatoes
  Boiling water
- ½ pound green beans (ends removed), cut into 2-inch lengths
- ¾ pound asparagus (tough ends removed), cut into slanting slices about ½-inch thick
- 1 pound peas (shelled) or 1 package (10 oz.) frozen peas
  Butter or red leaf lettuce
- 2 cans (about 7 oz. *each*) tuna, drained
- 1 small red onion, thinly sliced
- 3 large tomatoes, cut in wedges
- 2 hard-cooked eggs, sliced
  About 1 dozen pitted ripe olives
- 3 or 4 anchovy fillets (optional)
  Creamy Dijon dressing (directions follow)

Place potatoes in 1 inch boiling water; cover and cook just until tender when pierced (about 20 minutes). Lift out potatoes with slotted spoon and cool quickly under cold running water and drain. Cut into ¾-inch cubes.

Cook beans, covered, in the boiling water until just barely tender (about 10 minutes); cool quickly under cold running water and drain.

Place asparagus in enough boiling water to cover. Cook, covered, over medium-high heat until tender (about 8 minutes); drain and cool under cold running water and drain again.

Place fresh peas in 1 inch boiling water. Cover and cook over medium-high heat until tender (about 5 minutes); drain and cool under cold running water and drain again. (If using frozen peas, do not cook.)

Line a large shallow salad bowl with lettuce leaves. Distribute potatoes, beans, asparagus, and peas over bottom; cover with a layer of tuna chunks. Arrange onion, tomato, egg, olives, and anchovies (if used) over top. Cover and refrigerate until thoroughly chilled or until next day. Prepare dressing, cover and chill.

To serve, pour dressing over salad and toss. Makes 6 servings.

Creamy Dijon dressing. In a blender combine 2 **hard-cooked eggs** (sliced), 4 canned **anchovy fillets** (drained), 2 cloves **garlic**, ½ cup **olive oil** or salad oil, ⅓ cup **white wine vinegar**, ¼ cup **whipping cream**, 3 tablespoons **Dijon mustard**, 1 tablespoon **prepared horseradish**, 1 teaspoon **sugar**; whirl until smooth. Add **salt** and **pepper** to taste.

Piquant Carrot Salad

A lively sweet-tart dressing flavors crisp carrots, green pepper, and onion. As a make-ahead vegetable salad, it's easy to transport to a picnic or potluck supper.

- 1½ pounds carrots (about 8 medium-size), cut into ¼-inch-thick slanting slices
  Boiling water
- 1 medium-size onion, cut into ¼-inch-thick rings
- 1 small green pepper, cut into ¼-inch-thick rings
- ¼ cup white wine vinegar
- 3 tablespoons *each* sugar and salad oil
- 1 tablespoon catsup
- ½ teaspoon *each* seasoned salt, celery seed, Worcestershire, and Dijon mustard

In a pan over medium-high heat, cook carrots, covered, in 1 inch boiling water just until tender when pierced (about 5 minutes). Drain, cool quickly under cold running water; drain again. In a serving bowl, layer carrots, onion rings, and pepper rings.

Combine vinegar, sugar, oil, catsup, salt, celery seed, Worcestershire, and mustard; blend well and pour over carrot mixture.

Cover and refrigerate salad for at least 4 hours or until next day, stirring several times. Makes 4 to 6 servings.

Carrot-Raisin Slaw

A deli favorite over the years, a salad of shredded carrots dotted with raisins takes on even more appeal with the addition of sliced green onion and celery.

- 5 large carrots, shredded
- 1 cup thinly sliced celery
- ½ cup thinly sliced green onion
- ¾ cup raisins
- 4 tablespoons *each* sour cream and mayonnaise
- 1 tablespoon lemon juice
- ½ teaspoon salt
  Dash of pepper

In a salad bowl, mix together carrots, celery, onion, and raisins. In a small bowl, combine sour cream, mayonnaise, lemon juice, salt, and pepper; blend well. Add to vegetables and toss well. Cover and refrigerate for at least an hour or until next day. Makes 4 to 6 servings.

TENDER SPINACH LEAVES contrast with crunchy cauliflower slices for a sturdy green salad that won't wilt readily. Garnish with toasted almonds and avocado slices. The recipe is on page 12.

Hot Salad Showmanship

Few things add more flair to a dinner than a course skillfully prepared at the table. Restaurant chefs capitalize on this with hot salads, heating voluminous amounts of spinach, romaine, cabbage, or iceberg lettuce until they quickly wilt to a tender green mass.

With a little organization and a chafing dish, you can do the same thing at home. If you don't have a chafing dish with its own heat source, an electric wok or frying pan will work as well.

Some of the cooking can be done in the kitchen to be repeated briefly at the table just before serving. Assemble the utensils and ingredients ahead of time and have them close at hand, as the whole process goes very quickly.

Wilted Lettuce with Browned Butter Dressing

Unlike most wilted lettuce dressings, this one has no vinegar. The proper assembly and arranging of the salad is important so that you can pour the foaming browned butter dressing directly onto the green onions to cook them slightly before you mix the salad. You can choose between red leaf and butter lettuce.

    1   medium-size head butter or
          red leaf lettuce
    2   medium-size tomatoes, cut into thin
          wedges and seeded
    1/8 teaspoon *each* salt and pepper
    3   green onions with 2 inches of green
          tops, thinly sliced
    1   tablespoon sesame seed
    5   tablespoons butter

Break lettuce coarsely into salad bowl; place tomatoes on top. Sprinkle lettuce and tomatoes with salt and pepper. Place onion slices in center of salad.

In a small frying pan over medium heat, toast sesame seed, stirring, until lightly brown. Add butter and continue to cook over medium heat until mixture foams and lightly browns (do not let it burn). Pour hot sesame-butter over salad; mix lightly. Makes 4 servings.

Hot Spinach Salad with Bacon

The seasonings are simple and delicious for this salad—bacon and some of the drippings, mustard, vinegar, salt, and pepper. You do some quick mixing of the ingredients over the heat just before serving.

    5   strips bacon, cut in 3/4-inch pieces
    1 1/2 tablespoons red wine vinegar
    1/4 teaspoon *each* sugar and dry mustard
    1   bunch (about 1 1/4 lbs.) spinach, broken
          into bite-size pieces
        Salt and pepper

In the kitchen, cook bacon in chafing dish or frying pan over medium-high heat until crisp. Remove from heat, lift out bacon, and drain; crumble bacon into a small bowl. Discard all but 2 tablespoons drippings.

Combine vinegar, sugar, and mustard in a small bowl; blend well.

At the table, place chafing dish over high heat to warm bacon drippings. Place 1/2 the spinach in chafing dish and mix gently, lifting greens from pan bottom to coat leaves with drippings. As spinach wilts, add more greens and toss to coat leaves evenly. Add vinegar mixture to spinach and season with salt and pepper to taste; sprinkle bacon over and serve. Makes about 4 servings.

Hot Cabbage Slaw

Here's another salad best prepared in the kitchen to bring to the table to finish. This is hot cabbage slaw with a sweet-tart dressing.

    2   tablespoons *each* sugar and
          lemon juice
    1/2 teaspoon *each* Worcestershire and
          Dijon mustard
    2   teaspoons celery seed
    6   strips bacon, cut into 1/2-inch pieces
        Salad oil
    1   medium-size onion, chopped
    1   clove garlic, minced or pressed
    6   cups finely shredded cabbage
        Salt and pepper

Combine sugar, lemon juice, Worcestershire, mustard, and celery seed; set aside.

In the kitchen cook bacon in a frying pan over medium-high heat until crisp. Remove pan from heat, lift out bacon, and drain. Discard all but 1/4 cup of the drippings or add enough oil to make that amount; place in chafing dish.

At the table in a chafing dish, warm drippings over high heat; add onion and garlic and cook, stirring constantly, for 30 seconds. Add lemon juice mixture and heat until it boils, then add cabbage and turn off heat. Toss salad, add bacon, and toss again; add salt and pepper to taste. Serve on individual salad plates. Makes 4 to 6 servings.

Hot Iceberg-Chicory Salad

Browned slices of dry salami sprinkled throughout this heated green salad make it unusual.

- ¼ pound sliced dry salami, cut into ¼-inch strips
  Olive oil or salad oil
- 3 tablespoons wine vinegar
- 2 teaspoons sugar
- 1 teaspoon dry basil
  Salt and pepper
- 1 small red onion, thinly sliced
- 1 clove garlic, minced or pressed
- 1 small head *each* iceberg lettuce and chicory, broken into bite-size pieces
- 1 jar (4 oz.) diced pimentos, drained

In the kitchen, cook salami in a frying pan over medium-high heat, stirring frequently until lightly browned; remove from heat. Lift out salami and set aside. Add enough oil to pan drippings to make ¼ cup; place in chafing dish.

Combine vinegar, sugar, basil, and salt and pepper to taste; set aside.

At the table in a chafing dish, heat drippings over high heat; add onion and garlic and cook for 30 seconds, stirring continuously. Add vinegar mixture and heat until it boils. Add lettuce, chicory, and pimentos; immediately turn off heat. Toss salad; then add salami and salt and pepper to taste; mix again. Serve on individual salad plates. Makes 4 to 6 servings.

Escarole & Sausage Salad

For simplicity, fry bacon and sausage in the kitchen to reheat in a chafing dish at the table.

- ½ teaspoon sugar
- ¼ teaspoon dry mustard
- ⅛ teaspoon pepper
- 2 tablespoons red wine vinegar
- 3 strips bacon, cut into ¾-inch pieces
- 1 medium-size Polish sausage, sliced
- 1 medium-size head escarole, curly endive, or romaine broken into bite-size pieces

Combine sugar, mustard, pepper, and vinegar; set aside.

In the kitchen, cook bacon in chafing dish or frying pan over medium heat. When partially cooked, add sausage and cook until browned. Remove from heat, lift out bacon and sausage, drain, and set aside. Discard all but 3 tablespoons drippings.

At the table, place chafing dish with reserved drippings over low heat, add vinegar mixture, and heat, stirring, until blended and hot. Add greens, bacon, and sausage, and toss until evenly coated. Makes 4 servings.

Oriental Wilted Romaine Salad

A wok is ideal for stir-frying the crunchy croutons as well as for wilting the greens.

- 1 cup homemade croutons (see directions, page 69)
- 2 tablespoons lemon juice
- 1 tablespoon *each* sugar and catsup
- ½ teaspoon *each* Worcestershire and Dijon mustard
- ¼ cup salad oil
- 1 medium-size onion, chopped
- 1 small bunch (¾ lb.) romaine, broken into bite-size pieces
- ¼ pound bean sprouts

Prepare croutons; set aside. Mix lemon juice, sugar, catsup, Worcestershire, and mustard; set aside.

Heat oil in a wok or wide frying pan over high heat; add onion and cook, stirring, for 30 seconds. Add lemon juice mixture and when it boils, add romaine and remove from heat. Add sprouts, mix well, then turn into a bowl; top with croutons. Makes about 4 servings.

Pineapple Wilted Lettuce

A basic wilted salad takes on a new dimension with the addition of sweet chunks of pineapple.

- 1 medium-size head butter or red leaf lettuce
- ⅔ cup pineapple chunks (fresh or canned and drained)
- 4 strips bacon, cut into ½-inch pieces
  About ¼ cup wine vinegar
- 2 tablespoons water
- ¼ teaspoon salt

Break lettuce coarsely into a salad bowl; add pineapple chunks.

In a small frying pan over medium heat, cook bacon until crisp. Add vinegar, water, and salt to bacon and drippings. Bring to a boil, stirring constantly, for about 2 minutes until dressing is slightly reduced.

Pour hot dressing over lettuce and pineapple. Cover bowl and let stand for about 30 seconds; then toss salad lightly. Serve immediately. Makes about 4 servings.

Swiss Cheese-Vegetable Salad

Matchstick-size pieces of Swiss cheese are tossed with crunchy vegetables.

- 12 ounces Swiss cheese, cut in matchstick-size pieces
- 2 large green peppers, cut into thin, 2-inch-long strips
- 2 green onions, thinly sliced
- 3 stalks celery, thinly sliced
- 3 or 4 carrots, shredded
- 1 jar (4 oz.) sliced pimentos, drained
- ¾ cup coarsely chopped smoked, salted, roasted almonds
- 1 cup sour cream or unflavored yogurt
- 2 tablespoons Dijon mustard
- 4 drops liquid hot pepper seasoning
  Salt and pepper

In a salad bowl, mix together cheese, peppers, onion, celery, carrots, pimentos, and almonds.

Combine sour cream, mustard, hot pepper seasoning, and salt and pepper to taste; blend well. Pour over vegetables and toss to blend. Makes 4 servings.

Fresh Asparagus Victor

Whole asparagus spears substitute for celery in this springtime version of the famous marinated salad originated by Chef Victor Hirtzler of the St. Francis Hotel in San Francisco.

- 1 can (about 14 oz.) regular-strength chicken broth
- 2 pounds asparagus, tough ends removed
- 6 tablespoons olive oil or salad oil
- 4 tablespoons white wine vinegar
- 2 tablespoons *each* finely chopped green onion and pimento
- 1 teaspoon Dijon mustard
- ¼ teaspoon salt
- ⅛ teaspoon pepper
  Shredded iceberg lettuce
- 2 hard-cooked eggs, quartered
- 8 to 12 cherry tomatoes, halved
  Pitted ripe olives
- 1 can (2 oz.) anchovy fillets, drained (optional)

In a large frying pan, heat chicken broth to boiling; add asparagus, reduce heat, cover, and simmer for

ITALIAN ANTIPASTO can be the salad before a meal, or it can be a light meal by itself. Diners choose from assorted raw and marinated vegetables, egg wedges, and tuna. Everything is dressed with a simple olive oil-vinegar dressing. The recipe is on page 8.

7 to 9 minutes or until tender when pierced. With tongs, remove asparagus to a deep bowl. (Save broth for other uses, if you wish.)

Combine olive oil, vinegar, onion, pimento, mustard, salt, and pepper; blend well. Pour dressing over asparagus; cover and refrigerate for 4 to 6 hours.

To serve, arrange shredded lettuce on a large platter. Place asparagus on top in several piles; garnish with eggs, tomatoes, olives, and anchovies, if desired. Drizzle remaining dressing over all. Makes 4 to 6 servings.

Tossed Avocado & Celery Salad

Mix this crisp-and-creamy salad gently to avoid mashing the avocado pieces. Garnish with watercress sprigs.

- ½ cup mayonnaise
- 2 tablespoons Dijon mustard
- ¼ teaspoon salt
- ⅛ teaspoon pepper
- 2 large avocados
- 4 cups thinly sliced celery
- 2 green onions, thinly sliced
  Watercress sprigs

In a bowl, combine mayonnaise, mustard, salt, and pepper. Peel, pit, and cube avocados; add to dressing. Gently stir in celery and onion. Turn into a serving dish and garnish with watercress. Makes 4 servings.

Celery Root Salad Rémoulade

Beneath the wrinkled brown skin of the celery root (also called celeriac) lies smooth white flesh known for its distinctive crisp texture and subtle celery flavor. The cut surface darkens quickly unless the celery root is cooked, covered with water, or coated with an acidic sauce.

- 5 tablespoons olive oil or salad oil
- 2 tablespoons Dijon mustard
- 1½ tablespoons vinegar
- ½ teaspoon salt
- ⅛ teaspoon liquid hot pepper seasoning
- 1 tablespoon paprika
- 1 hard-cooked egg yolk
- 2 pounds celery root (about 3 medium-size)
  Lettuce leaves
  Chopped parsley

In a blender, combine olive oil, mustard, vinegar, salt, hot pepper seasoning, paprika, and egg yolk; whirl until smooth.

(Continued on next page)

Cut off and discard top from celery root; with a vegetable peeler, peel away and discard thick outer skin. Wash root, cut into matchstick-size pieces, and mix into rémoulade sauce. Cover and refrigerate for at least 2 hours or until next day.

To serve, lift celery root from sauce and let drain briefly. Mound in a lettuce-lined serving dish and sprinkle with chopped parsley. Makes 4 servings.

Sprout & Tomato Salad

An iceberg lettuce, tomato, and crunchy bean sprout salad lends itself to the addition of a little shrimp, crab, or shredded chicken, if you like.

> 2 tablespoons sesame seed
> 2 cups *each* bean sprouts and shredded iceberg lettuce
> ⅓ cup thinly sliced celery
> 3 green onions, thinly sliced
> 1 cup cherry tomatoes, halved
> ¼ pound small cooked shrimp, crab meat, or shredded cooked chicken (optional)
> Oil-vinegar dressing (directions follow)

In a frying pan over low heat, toast sesame seed until golden (about 2 minutes), shaking pan frequently; set aside.

In a salad bowl, mix together sprouts, lettuce, celery, onion, tomatoes, and shrimp (if used). Make oil-vinegar dressing as directed.

Sprinkle sesame seed over vegetable mixture, add dressing, and toss gently but thoroughly. Makes 4 servings.

Oil-vinegar dressing. Blend 3 tablespoons **salad oil**, 2 tablespoons *each* **cider vinegar** and **soy sauce**, 1 tablespoon **sugar**, ¼ teaspoon **salt**, and dash of **pepper**.

Sliced Tomatoes with Herb Dressing

Basil and tarragon are great flavor companions to tomatoes. Serve slices of big beefsteak tomatoes by the plateful, flavored with a simple dressing made with one of these herbs.

> ¼ cup olive oil or salad oil (or half of each)
> 2 tablespoons garlic vinegar or red wine vinegar
> ½ teaspoon *each* salt and sugar
> ¼ cup fresh basil, finely chopped, or 1 tablespoon dry basil (or 1 teaspoon tarragon leaves and 2 teaspoons chives)
> 2 or 3 beefsteak tomatoes, peeled and cut in ¼-inch-thick slices
> 1 large red onion, thinly sliced (optional)
> Pepper

Combine oil, vinegar, salt, sugar, and basil. Blend well and set aside for 1 to 2 hours to mellow flavors. Overlap tomato slices in a shallow bowl; tuck a few onion slices in between, if you wish. Drizzle dressing over tomatoes; serve or refrigerate for up to 1 hour. (If refrigerated, spoon dressing from bottom of bowl over tomatoes before serving.) Sprinkle pepper over top. Makes 4 to 6 servings.

Tomato Stuffed with Vegetable Cottage Cheese Salad

For a wholesome, low-cal luncheon, serve cottage cheese salad nestled in peeled, hollowed-out tomato or bell pepper halves and garnished with hard-cooked egg.

> 1 pint small curd low-fat cottage cheese
> 2 tablespoons chopped parsley
> ½ cup thinly sliced green onion
> ¼ cup chopped green or red bell pepper
> ⅓ cup chopped celery
> ½ cup chopped radishes and shredded carrot
> ½ teaspoon *each* garlic salt, dill weed, and dry mustard
> Spinach or lettuce leaves
> 2 large tomatoes or green or red bell peppers
> Paprika

Combine cottage cheese, parsley, onion, bell pepper, celery, radishes, carrot, garlic salt, dill weed, and mustard. Cover and chill for at least 1 hour or until next day.

To serve, line 4 salad plates with spinach leaves. Cut tomatoes or peppers in half and scoop out pulp or seeds. Place a half on each plate; fill with equal portions of cheese mixture. Sprinkle with paprika. Makes 4 servings.

Marinated Artichokes with Mint

For an attractive buffet salad that stays fresh and crisp for hours, try this artichoke recipe. The artichoke hearts are arranged on a round platter in circles within circles, then garnished with fresh mint sprigs in the center.

> 2 packages (9 oz. *each*) frozen artichoke hearts, thawed
> ⅔ cup salad oil
> ⅓ cup white wine vinegar
> ½ teaspoon *each* dry mustard and sugar
> 1 teaspoon salt
> ¼ teaspoon pepper
> 3 tablespoons chopped fresh mint or 1½ tablespoons dry mint leaves
> Fresh mint sprigs (optional)

Cook artichokes according to package directions; drain.

In a small bowl, combine oil, vinegar, mustard, sugar, salt, pepper, and mint; blend well. Pour over artichokes. Cover and refrigerate for at least 4 hours or until next day.

To serve, arrange artichokes, cut side up, on a platter. Lightly spoon over some dressing to moisten. Garnish with mint sprigs, if desired. Makes 8 servings.

Portable Picnic Salad
(recipe below)

Portable Picnic Salad

Readily available frozen vegetables are the basis of this portable salad, perfect for packing into a plastic container and toting to a picnic.

- 1 package (10 oz.) frozen Brussels sprouts, thawed
- 1 package (10 oz.) frozen cauliflower clusters, thawed
- ½ cup *each* chopped green pepper and sliced green onion
- ⅓ cup white wine vinegar
- 3 tablespoons olive oil or salad oil
- ½ teaspoon *each* salt, dry mustard, and sugar
- ¼ teaspoon *each* paprika and tarragon leaves
- ⅛ teaspoon pepper
- 1 can (14½ oz.) sliced baby tomatoes, well drained

Cut Brussels sprouts in half lengthwise; also cut any large cauliflowerets in half lengthwise. Place vegetables in a steamer basket; set basket in a kettle over 1 inch of boiling water. Cover and steam for 2 to 3 minutes or until vegetables are tender-crisp; place in a bowl with green pepper and onion.

In a small bowl, combine vinegar, oil, salt, mustard, sugar, paprika, tarragon, and pepper; blend well. Pour over hot vegetables, stirring gently to coat. Cover and refrigerate for at least 4 hours or until next day.

Before serving, add tomatoes to salad and toss gently. Makes 4 to 6 servings.

Mushroom, Blue Cheese & Walnut Salad

Chunks of zesty blue cheese and crunchy walnuts garnish this marinated fresh mushroom salad.

- ¼ cup olive oil or salad oil
- 2 teaspoons dry basil
- ½ teaspoon salt
- ⅛ teaspoon *each* pepper and paprika
- 2 teaspoons Dijon mustard
- 4 teaspoons white wine vinegar
- 1 teaspoon lemon juice
- ½ pound mushrooms, sliced
- ½ cup thinly sliced green onion, including some green tops
- ¾ cup broken walnut pieces (optional)
- About 4 ounces blue-veined cheese, coarsely crumbled
- 3 cups bite-size pieces of chicory (curly endive), romaine, or butter lettuce leaves
- About 6 cherry tomatoes, whole or halved

In a salad bowl, combine oil, basil, salt, pepper, paprika, mustard, vinegar, and lemon juice. Beat with a fork until blended. Mix in mushrooms and green onion; let stand at room temperature to marinate for about 1 hour or until serving time.

Mix in walnut pieces, blue cheese, chicory, and cherry tomatoes. Or serve mushrooms on individual lettuce-lined plates and garnish with walnut pieces, blue cheese, and cherry tomatoes. Makes 2 servings.

Chilled Mushroom Bowl

This is a get-up-and-go salad that travels well for long distances. Mushroom slices can marinate as long as overnight. Just before serving, toss in watercress sprigs.

- ½ cup pine nuts or slivered almonds
- 1 pound mushrooms, sliced
- 1 large red or green bell pepper, seeded and cut into thin strips
- ½ cup olive oil or salad oil
- 2 tablespoons *each* lemon juice and white wine vinegar
- ½ teaspoon tarragon leaves
- 1 bunch watercress

Spread pine nuts in a shallow pan and toast in a 350° oven for 8 minutes or until lightly browned; turn into a bowl. Add mushrooms and pepper.

(Continued on next page)

...*Chilled Mushroom Bowl (cont'd.)*

Combine oil, lemon juice, vinegar, and tarragon; blend well, pour over mushrooms, and mix well. Cover and refrigerate for several hours or until next day.

To serve, stir in watercress sprigs. Makes 6 to 8 servings.

Zucchini Stick Salad

Zucchini is so prolific, it makes a perfect salad for the summer gardener. Lightly cooked zucchini and bell pepper sticks stay tender-crisp while marinating in a zesty caper dressing.

- 2 tablespoons olive oil or salad oil
- 1½ pounds zucchini (about 6 medium-size), cut into ¼ by 3-inch strips
- 2 medium-size red or green bell peppers, cut into ¼ by 3-inch strips
- ½ cup *each* halved ripe olives and sliced green onion
- 1 teaspoon garlic salt
- ½ teaspoon pepper
- 3 tablespoons *each* capers and white wine vinegar
- ¼ cup salad oil
- ½ teaspoon *each* oregano leaves and sugar

Heat oil in a wide frying pan over medium heat. Add zucchini and pepper and stir to coat with oil; cover and cook until tender-crisp (5 to 7 minutes). Remove from heat and stir in olives, onion, garlic salt, and pepper. Turn into a salad bowl.

In a small bowl, combine capers, vinegar, oil, oregano, and sugar. Add to zucchini mixture and toss gently to coat. Cover and refrigerate for at least 3 hours or until next day. Makes about 6 servings.

Stacked Guacamole Salad

Popular Mexican tostadas can be simplified if you use purchased tortilla chips instead of frying the tortillas yourself.

- Guacamole dressing (directions follow)
- 1 small head iceberg lettuce, shredded
- 1 medium-size zucchini, thinly sliced
- 1 can (15 oz.) refried beans
- ¼ teaspoon garlic powder
- 1½ cups shredded Cheddar cheese
- ¼ pound mushrooms, sliced
- ½ cup sliced radishes
- ½ cup salted, roasted sunflower seeds
- 4 to 6 cherry tomatoes
- About 1 dozen tortilla chips
- Taco sauce (optional)

Make guacamole dressing and set aside.

Pile lettuce on 2 large plates. Top with a layer of zucchini slices. In a pan over low heat, place beans and garlic powder and heat, stirring, until hot and bubbly. Spoon half the beans over each salad, cover with half the cheese, mushrooms, and radishes. Top each with half the guacamole; sprinkle with sunflower seeds. Garnish with tomatoes and tortilla chips. If desired, pass taco sauce to spoon over individual servings. Makes 2 servings.

Guacamole dressing. Peel, pit, and mash 1 medium-size **avocado**. Mix avocado with 2 tablespoons **lemon juice**, ¼ teaspoon **garlic powder**, 2 tablespoons chopped fresh **coriander** (or 1 tablespoon dry cilantro leaves), ¼ cup chopped **green onion**, and 2 to 4 tablespoons diced canned **California green chiles**. Add **salt** to taste.

Broccoli-Cheddar Cheese Salad

Pictured on facing page

Broccoli is quickly steamed and chilled to mix with yellow Cheddar cheese to make a beautiful salad accented with slices of mushrooms and a dressing of chives and toasted pine nuts.

- ¾ pound broccoli
- Boiling water
- 2 tablespoons pine nuts
- 4 ounces Cheddar cheese, cut in matchstick-size pieces
- ¼ pound medium-size mushrooms, thinly sliced
- Chive dressing (directions follow)
- Radishes (optional)

Trim off broccoli stem ends and peel outer layer of stalks. Cut flowerets from stalks and cut stalks crosswise into thin slices. Place flowerets and sliced stalks in a steamer basket; set in a kettle over 1 inch of boiling water. Cook, covered, until barely tender when pierced (about 5 minutes); drain, rinse under cold water, and drain again.

Meanwhile, place pine nuts in a frying pan over medium-low heat and cook, stirring, until golden (about 5 minutes).

To serve, gently mix together in a salad bowl, broccoli, cheese, mushrooms, and dressing, coating vegetables well. Sprinkle with toasted pine nuts and garnish with radishes, if you wish. Makes 4 servings.

Chive dressing. Combine 4 tablespoons **olive oil** or salad oil, 3 tablespoons **lemon juice**, 2 tablespoons minced **chives** or green onion, ¼ teaspoon *each* **garlic salt** and **dry mustard**, and ⅛ teaspoon **white pepper**.

A VISUAL DELIGHT, this mixture of bright green broccoli, golden Cheddar pieces, and snowy white mushroom slices is bathed in a tart chive-lemon dressing. Sprinkle toasted pine nuts over top. The recipe is on this page.

chpt. 2 goes from pg 32 to 51...

Poultry, Seafood & Meat Salads

These high-protein salads are substantial enough to do main-dish duty, adaptable enough to be paired with an entrée. And thanks to already-cooked meats, they go together quickly.

Guacamole & Chicken Salad

Festive Mexican-style chicken salad can be chilled ahead, ready for fast assembly several hours before serving. Plan to use leftover meat from a roast turkey or chicken or buy a barbecued broiler-fryer.

    1 medium-size head iceberg lettuce
    3 tablespoons olive oil or salad oil
 1½ tablespoons white wine vinegar
    2 tablespoons chopped canned green chiles
    1 tablespoon chopped shallot or green onion
    3 cups diced cold cooked chicken or turkey
   ⅓ cup sour cream
      Guacamole (directions follow)
   ½ cup (2 oz.) shredded jack cheese
      Pitted ripe olives, cherry tomatoes, and
        sweet red cherry peppers

Arrange outer leaves of lettuce in a shallow serving bowl. Shred remaining lettuce. In a large bowl, mix together oil, vinegar, chiles, and shallot; add shredded lettuce and toss lightly. Spoon into lettuce-lined bowl and arrange chicken on top. Spread with sour cream and cover with a layer of guacamole. Sprinkle with cheese and garnish with olives, tomatoes, and peppers.

Cover and refrigerate for as long as 2 hours. Makes 4 servings.

Guacamole. Peel and pit 1 large **avocado;** cut in chunks and place in blender. Add ¼ teaspoon **salt,** ¼ cup **sour cream,** and 1 clove **garlic;** whirl until smooth.

Curried Chicken on Pineapple Rings

Curry-flavored yogurt makes a low-cal dressing to pour over a chicken and fruit mixture set on pineapple rings. Garnish with chopped peanuts, almonds, or cashews.

1 cup unflavored yogurt
3 tablespoons finely chopped Major
  Grey's chutney
1 teaspoon *each* curry powder and
  ground coriander
¾ teaspoon garlic salt
½ teaspoon dry mustard
  Dash of cayenne
2 small bananas
3 cups diced cold cooked chicken or turkey
1 small green pepper, coarsely chopped
1 can (11 oz.) mandarin oranges, well drained
½ cup raisins
¼ cup thinly sliced green onion
1 large pineapple (about 5 lbs.)
  Butter lettuce leaves
½ cup coarsely chopped salted peanuts,
  almonds, or cashews

Combine yogurt, chutney, curry powder, coriander, garlic salt, mustard, and cayenne; blend well
and set aside.

Cut bananas into ¼-inch slices; combine with
chicken, pepper, oranges, raisins, and onion.

Peel and core pineapple. Cutting crosswise, slice
off 6 thick (about ¾ inch) rounds; set aside. Cut
remaining pineapple into bite-size chunks (you
should have about 1 cup); drain and add to chicken
mixture.

Pour curry-yogurt dressing over chicken mixture and toss gently.

Arrange lettuce leaves on 6 salad plates, then
lay a pineapple ring on each. Top pineapple slices
with equal amounts of salad mixture. Sprinkle
each serving with nuts. Makes 6 servings.

BLT Chicken Salad

A salad version of the bacon-lettuce-tomato sandwich features chicken topped with tangy herb
dressing.

  Parsley-herb dressing (directions follow)
1 medium-size head iceberg lettuce,
  shredded
1 medium-size avocado
3 cups shredded cold cooked chicken
½ pound bacon, crisply cooked
  and crumbled
2 large tomatoes, peeled, seeded, and diced

Make dressing, cover, and chill for several hours.

Place shredded lettuce in a salad bowl. Peel,
pit, and slice avocado and place on lettuce with
the chicken, bacon, tomatoes, and avocado. Pour
over dressing, toss well, and serve. Makes 4 to 6
servings.

Parsley-herb dressing. In a jar, combine ½ cup
salad oil, ¼ cup **white wine vinegar**, 1 teaspoon
salt, 2 teaspoons **sugar**, ¾ teaspoon **pepper**, 1¼

teaspoons **dry mustard**, 1 clove **garlic** (minced
or pressed), and ⅓ cup finely chopped **parsley**;
blend well.

Chicken in Cantaloupe with Curry Dressing

A dressing flavored with peanut butter, curry,
and soy sauce gives this salad a Far Eastern flavor.
Use melon shells as containers for the chicken and
cantaloupe mixture; top with peanuts.

2 medium-size cantaloupes
2 to 3 cups cold cooked chicken, cut in
  bite-size pieces
¼ cup *each* thinly sliced celery and
  green onion
¼ cup seeded and diced red or green bell
  pepper
  Curry-peanut dressing (directions follow)
  Lettuce leaves
¼ cup chopped salted peanuts

Cut each cantaloupe in half; scoop out and discard
seeds. Remove melon fruit with a melon ball cutter
leaving about ¼ inch of the fruit next to the rind.
Set melon balls and hollow shells aside to drain.

Mix together chicken, celery, onion, and pepper. Prepare curry-peanut dressing and stir into
chicken mixture along with melon balls. Cover and
refrigerate.

To serve, arrange lettuce leaves on 4 salad plates
and place 1 melon shell on each. Spoon mixture
into melon shells and top each with nuts. Makes
4 servings.

Curry-peanut dressing. In a blender, combine
⅓ cup *each* **peanut butter, mayonnaise,** and **sour
cream;** 2 tablespoons **lime juice;** 1 clove **garlic;** 1
teaspoon **curry powder;** and ¼ teaspoon *each*
ground ginger and **soy sauce.** Whirl until smooth.
Add **salt** and **pepper** to taste.

Meat—How Many Pounds for How Many Cups?

Most of our recipes will call for so many cups
of cold cooked chicken, beef, ham, or turkey.
If you have no leftovers handy, you can pur-
chase and cook meats just for the salads or
buy cooked meat from a delicatessen.

A 3-pound broiler-fryer chicken will give
you about 3 cups meat. A 1-pound whole
chicken breast will give you about 1½ cups
meat. And ½ pound cooked boneless ham,
beef, or turkey yields about 2 cups meat.

Chicken-stuffed Melon with Pomegranate

Pictured on facing page

For a visual treat, fill hollowed-out cantaloupe halves with chicken salad and top with green grapes and crimson pomegranate seeds. Pour over a lime and honey dressing just before serving.

- 2 medium-size cantaloupes
- 2 cups diced cold cooked chicken
- ½ cup seedless grapes
  Seeds from 1 pomegranate
- 1 small kiwi, sliced (optional)
  Lime-honey dressing (directions follow)

Cut each cantaloupe in half making zigzag cuts. Scoop out and discard seeds. With curved grapefruit knife remove melon fruit and cut into bite-size pieces; drain melon pieces and shells. Mix melon pieces with chicken and spoon equal portions into empty shells. Top with grapes and pomegranate seeds. Garnish with sliced kiwi, if desired. Prepare lime-honey dressing, pour over, and serve. Makes 4 servings.

Lime-honey dressing. Mix together 4 tablespoons *each* **lime juice** and **honey** with ¼ teaspoon *each* **ground coriander** and **nutmeg**.

Asparagus-Tarragon Chicken Salad

Asparagus spears, citrus fruit, and avocado combine with half a tarragon-poached chicken breast in this dinner salad.

- 2 whole chicken breasts
  (about 1 lb. *each*), split
- ½ cup water
- 1 teaspoon chicken-seasoned stock base
- ½ teaspoon tarragon leaves
- 1 medium-size grapefruit
- 2 medium-size oranges
- 1 medium-size avocado
- 1 tablespoon lemon juice
- 1 medium-size head romaine
- 1 pound fresh asparagus spears, cooked
  and chilled, or 1 can (16 oz.) asparagus
  spears, drained
  Citrus dressing (directions follow)

In a wide frying pan, place chicken breasts, water, stock base, and tarragon; cover and simmer for 15

CRIMSON POMEGRANATE SEEDS garnish salads of chicken, fruit, and honey-lime dressing handsomely served in the hollows of cantaloupe halves. The recipe is on this page.

minutes. Drain, skin, and bone chicken, keeping breasts in one piece; then refrigerate.

Meanwhile, remove peel and white membrane from grapefruit and oranges; reserve orange peel. Lift out sections. Peel, pit, and slice avocado; sprinkle with lemon juice. Arrange outer leaves of romaine on 4 dinner plates. Break inner leaves into bite-size pieces and pile in center of plates. Place a chilled half chicken breast on each plate. Then add equal amounts of grapefruit and orange segments, avocado slices, and asparagus spears. Pass citrus dressing to spoon over. Makes 4 servings.

Citrus dressing. In a jar, combine ¼ cup *each* **mayonnaise** and **sour cream**, 1 teaspoon *each* **grated orange peel** and **lemon peel**, 1 tablespoon **lemon juice**, 1 teaspoon **sugar**, and 2 ounces **blue cheese** or Roquefort (crumbled).

Chinese Chicken Salad

Many variations of this salad vie for popularity. This one, without the traditional crisp noodles, is simpler than most; and the chicken roasts in a soy-sherry mixture for distinctive flavor.

- 2 tablespoons soy sauce
- 1 tablespoon *each* salad oil and sherry
- 1 clove garlic, minced or pressed
- ¼ teaspoon *each* ground ginger and Chinese
  five-spice or ground cinnamon
- 2½ to 3-pound broiler-fryer, cut in half
- ¼ cup sesame seed
  About 6 cups thinly shredded iceberg
  lettuce
- 3 green onions, thinly sliced
- 1 small bunch fresh coriander (cilantro),
  coarsely chopped
- 1 cup chopped salted cashews or
  peanuts
  Lemon dressing (directions follow)
  Salt and pepper

Mix together soy, salad oil, sherry, garlic, ginger, and five-spice. Rub mixture over chicken halves, coating thoroughly. Place chicken, skin side up, in a shallow baking pan. Pour over any extra soy mixture. Bake in a 400° oven until meat near bone is no longer pink when slashed (about 45 minutes). Cool, skin, bone, and cut chicken into thin strips.

Spread sesame seed in a frying pan over medium-high heat and toast, stirring, until golden (about 4 minutes).

In a salad bowl, mix together chicken, lettuce, onion, and coriander. Add sesame seed and ¾ cup of the nuts. Prepare lemon dressing, pour over chicken mixture, and toss lightly. Add salt and pepper to taste. Top with remaining nuts. Makes 4 to 6 servings.

(Continued on next page)

Lemon dressing. Combine ½ teaspoon **dry mustard**, 1 teaspoon *each* **sugar** and **grated lemon peel**, 2 teaspoons **soy sauce**, 1 tablespoon **lemon juice**, and 4 tablespoons **salad oil**.

Citrus Chicken Salad

Wheels of orange slices garnish this refreshing main dish salad. It's a good choice for a spring luncheon.

- 2 **large oranges**
- 4 **cups diced cold cooked chicken**
- ¾ **cup thinly sliced celery**
- ⅓ **cup** *each* **chopped green onion and green pepper**
- ½ **cup** *each* **sour cream and mayonnaise**
- 1 **tablespoon** *each* **lemon juice and sugar**
  Salt and pepper
- ½ **cup slivered almonds**
  Lettuce leaves

Grate 1 teaspoon orange peel from 1 orange; set peel aside. Then peel oranges, removing white membrane, and slice oranges crosswise into thin wheels. Cover and refrigerate. Mix together chicken, celery, green onion, and green pepper. Combine sour cream, mayonnaise, lemon juice, sugar, grated orange peel, and salt and pepper to taste; blend well. Stir into chicken mixture, cover, and chill for 2 to 3 hours.

Spread almonds on a shallow baking sheet and toast in a 350° oven for about 8 minutes or until golden.

Arrange lettuce leaves on a serving platter. Mound chicken salad on greens; arrange orange slices around outside edge of salad. Sprinkle with toasted almonds. Makes 4 servings.

Citrus Chicken Salad (recipe above)

Hoisin Chicken Salad

Hoisin sauce—a thick concoction of soy beans, garlic, and spices—is a classic accompaniment for Chinese Peking duck, although it accompanies chicken in this salad. Look for hoisin sauce in Oriental markets.

- ¼ **cup sesame seed**
- 6 **cups broken iceberg lettuce leaves**
- ⅓ **cup thinly sliced green onion**
- 2 **medium-size tomatoes, cut in thin wedges**
- 3 **cups shredded cold cooked chicken**
- ¼ **cup hoisin sauce**
- ¼ **cup lemon juice**
- ¼ **teaspoon ground ginger**
- ⅓ **cup salad oil**
  Garlic salt and pepper
  Cucumber slices

Spread sesame seed in a frying pan over medium-high heat; cook, stirring often, until golden (about 4 minutes); set aside.

In a salad bowl, mix together lettuce, green onion, tomatoes, and chicken; cover and refrigerate for 2 to 4 hours.

Meanwhile, combine hoisin sauce, lemon juice, ginger, and salad oil; blend well.

To serve, pour dressing over lettuce mixture, sprinkle sesame seed over all, and toss well. Season to taste with garlic salt and pepper. Garnish with cucumber slices. Makes 6 servings.

Chef's Coleslaw Salad

Coleslaw can become a chef's-style whole-meal salad with the addition of julienne meat and cheese strips. For variation, use curly-leaf savory, red cabbage, or Chinese (napa) cabbage.

- 5 **cups finely shredded cabbage**
- ½ **pound cooked ham, chicken, or tongue, cut in julienne strips, ¼ inch wide and 2 inches long (about 1½ cups)**
- 6 **ounces Cheddar, jack, or Swiss cheese, cut in julienne strips, ¼ inch wide and 2 inches long (about 1½ cups)**
- ½ **cup diced red onion**
- 1 **cup diced peeled cucumber**
- 2 **teaspoons caraway seed**
  Chef's dressing (directions follow)
  Sliced black olives

In a salad bowl, combine cabbage, ham, cheese, onion, cucumber, and caraway seed. Prepare dressing; pour over cabbage mixture and toss gently. Garnish with olives. Makes 4 servings.

Chef's dressing. Mix together ¾ cup **sour cream** or unflavored yogurt, ¼ cup **milk**, 2 tablespoons **cider vinegar**, ¼ teaspoon **pepper**, and 2 teaspoons *each* **seasoned salt, brown sugar,** and **Dijon mustard.**

Oriental Turkey Salad

Fresh lime juice sparks the dressing for turkey, bean sprouts, and celery cabbage salad.

    4 cups cubed cold cooked turkey
    2 cups cold cooked rice
    1 cup thinly sliced celery
    ½ cup thinly sliced green onion
    1 cup fresh bean sprouts
    ¾ cup mayonnaise
    ¼ cup lime juice
    1 clove garlic, minced or pressed
    1 tablespoon soy sauce
    2 teaspoons grated fresh ginger root
    1 teaspoon curry powder
    1 tablespoon finely chopped Major Grey's
       chutney
    3 cups shredded celery cabbage (also called
       Chinese or napa)

In a bowl, mix together turkey, rice, celery, all but 2 tablespoons of the green onion, and bean sprouts; cover and chill.

Combine mayonnaise, lime juice, garlic, soy, ginger, curry, and chutney; cover and chill.

To serve, pour dressing over turkey mixture and toss well. Line a large serving plate (or individual salad plates) with cabbage and mound turkey mixture on top; garnish with reserved green onion. Makes about 6 servings.

Green Pea & Salmon Salad

Accompany this colorful supper salad with crusty dinner rolls. The appearance of chilled cooked or canned salmon is enhanced if you carefully break it into large chunks.

    2 cups cold cooked salmon or 1 can (1 lb.)
       salmon, drained
    1 cup *each* frozen peas, thawed, and thinly
       sliced celery
    ¼ cup thinly sliced green onion
    4 hard-cooked eggs, diced
       Dill dressing (directions follow)
       Lettuce leaves
       Lemon wedges

Carefully separate salmon into large chunks; discard bones and skin, if necessary. Mix together salmon, peas, celery, green onion, and eggs; cover and refrigerate for 2 to 4 hours. Meanwhile, pre-

pare dill dressing; cover and refrigerate.

To serve, line 4 salad plates with lettuce leaves. Gently combine salmon mixture with dressing, then spoon evenly over greens and garnish with lemon wedges. Makes 4 servings.

Dill dressing. In a small bowl combine ⅔ cup **mayonnaise**, 2 tablespoons *each* **lemon juice** and finely chopped **dill pickle**, 1 teaspoon *each* **prepared mustard** and **dill weed**, and **salt** and **pepper** to taste.

Sardine Vegetable Salad

Sardines and egg wedges top a piquant salad of marinated potatoes, green beans, crisp cabbage, onion, pickle, and radishes.

    1 pound new potatoes
       Boiling water
       Lemon-mustard dressing
       (directions follow)
    1 pound green beans
    4 cups thinly sliced cabbage
    1 small red onion, thinly sliced
    ½ cup *each* chopped dill pickle and
       sliced radishes
       Salt and pepper
    2 or 3 cans (about 3¾ oz. *each*) sardines
       in oil, drained
    3 hard-cooked eggs, cut in wedges

Place potatoes in 1 inch boiling water; cover and cook until tender when pierced (about 30 minutes); lift from pan and let cool. Peel and thinly slice potatoes into a salad bowl. Prepare lemon dressing, pour over potatoes, and toss lightly to coat.

Remove stems and cut beans into 1-inch lengths; place in boiling water (adding more water, if necessary) and cook until tender-crisp (about 8 minutes). Cool under cold running water and drain; arrange on potatoes—don't mix. Cover and refrigerate for 2 to 6 hours.

Mix together cabbage, onion, pickle, and radishes; add to potatoes and beans. Toss lightly; add salt and pepper to taste. Arrange sardines and eggs on top. Makes about 6 servings.

(Continued on next page)

Lemon-mustard dressing. Combine ⅔ cup **salad oil;** ⅓ cup **lemon juice;** 2 teaspoons **Dijon mustard;** 1 teaspoon *each* **sugar, salt,** and **dry basil leaves;** ¼ teaspoon *each* **tarragon leaves** and **pepper;** and 1 clove **garlic,** minced or pressed.

Salmon Salad with Oranges

Having canned salmon in your cupboard makes last-minute dinners easy when preparing for two.

    1 can (about 8 oz.) salmon, drained
    1½ cups thinly sliced celery
    ⅓ cup thinly sliced green onion
    2 tablespoons finely chopped parsley
    5 tablespoons thinly sliced pimento-
         stuffed green olives
    2 large oranges
       Orange dressing (directions follow)
       Lettuce leaves

Break salmon into bite-size pieces; discard skin and bones. Combine salmon, celery, green onion, parsley, and 4 tablespoons of the olives. Remove peel and white membrane from oranges. Lift out orange sections and set a few aside for garnish; cut remaining sections in half and add to salmon mixture. Prepare orange dressing and pour over; toss lightly. Arrange lettuce leaves on 2 salad plates and mound half of the salmon mixture on each. Garnish with reserved orange sections and the remaining 1 tablespoon sliced olives. Makes 2 servings.

Orange dressing. Combine 3 tablespoons *each* **sour cream** and **mayonnaise,** 1 teaspoon *each* **Dijon mustard** and **prepared horseradish,** ½ teaspoon **garlic salt,** ⅛ teaspoon **pepper,** and 1 teaspoon **grated orange peel.**

Turbot Salad with Louis Dressing

This salad resembles Crab Louis, but less expensive Greenland turbot is used instead of crab.

    2 cups water
    3 lemon slices
    1 *each* medium-size onion and carrot,
         thickly sliced
    1 teaspoon salt
    ¼ teaspoon pepper
    2 cups thinly sliced celery
       About 2 pounds thawed Greenland turbot
         fillets or halibut fillets
       Louis dressing (directions follow)
    ⅓ cup finely chopped sweet pickle
       Romaine or iceberg lettuce
    3 hard-cooked eggs, quartered
       Cherry tomatoes

In a large frying pan, combine water, lemon, onion, carrot, salt, pepper, and ½ cup of the celery; bring to boiling, reduce heat, and simmer for 10 minutes. Push vegetables to one side of pan and place fish in pan, spooning some vegetables over fish. Return to boiling, cover, reduce heat, and simmer for 6 to 10 minutes or until thickest portions of fish flake readily when prodded with a fork. Remove from heat and chill fish in cooking liquid. Drain fish, discarding liquid (or reserve for fish stock), vegetables, and lemon. Pat fish dry and break into bite-size pieces (cover and refrigerate, if done ahead). Prepare Louis dressing.

To serve, gently mix together fish, pickle, the remaining 1½ cups celery, and about ¾ cup of the dressing. Line a serving platter with lettuce leaves and mound salad on top. Garnish with eggs and cherry tomatoes. Pass remaining dressing to spoon over servings. Makes 4 to 6 servings.

Louis dressing. In a small bowl, combine ½ cup *each* **mayonnaise** and **sour cream** with ⅓ cup **tomato-based chili sauce,** 1 tablespoon **lemon juice,** and 3 tablespoons chopped **green onion.**

California Shrimp Salad

Pictured on facing page

Shrimp and avocado, marinated in a vinegar-oil dressing, are served on a bed of shredded lettuce and topped with more of the tangy marinade.

    2 pounds medium-size shrimp
       Boiling water
    1 large avocado
       Green onion dressing (directions follow)
    1 large head iceberg lettuce, shredded

Place shrimp in a pan, cover with boiling water, and simmer for 5 to 8 minutes or until shrimp turn pink; shell and devein.

Peel, pit, and cube avocado. Place shrimp and avocado in a bowl. Prepare green onion dressing and pour over, gently turning to coat well. Cover and chill for 1 to 2 hours.

To serve, place shredded lettuce on a serving platter. With a slotted spoon, lift out shrimp-avocado mixture (reserve marinade) and mound onto lettuce, Pass reserved dressing to spoon over individual servings. Makes 6 to 8 servings.

Green onion dressing. Stir together ¼ cup **olive oil** or salad oil, ¼ cup **white wine vinegar,** 2 tablespoons **lemon juice,** ½ teaspoon **garlic salt,** ⅛ teaspoon **seasoned pepper,** and ½ cup minced **green onion.**

MARINATED WHOLE SHRIMP and chunks of avocado rest on a bed of shredded iceberg lettuce. Green onion in the tangy marinade adds color and zest. The recipe is on this page.

Crisp Shrimp Salad

A crisp, filling salad of small shrimp and fresh vegetables makes a hearty entrée.

>   1 **pound small cooked shrimp**
> ½ **pound mushrooms, thinly sliced**
>   1 **cup thinly sliced celery**
>   1 **cup finely chopped carrot**
> ½ **cup thinly sliced green onion**
>   1 **can (8 oz.) water chestnuts, drained and
>   sliced**
>   **Wine vinegar dressing (directions follow)**
>   **Lettuce leaves**
>   1 **large avocado**
>   **Cherry tomato halves**

Combine shrimp, mushrooms, celery, carrot, onion, and water chestnuts. Prepare dressing, pour over top, and mix well. Cover and refrigerate for at least 2 hours or as long as overnight (stir well several times).

To serve, arrange lettuce leaves on 6 salad plates. With a slotted spoon, lift shrimp mixture from dressing and mound on lettuce. Peel, pit, and slice avocado and use as garnish with tomato halves. Makes 6 servings.

Wine vinegar dressing. Mix together ½ cup **white wine vinegar,** 5 tablespoons **sugar,** 2 tablespoons **salad oil,** 1 tablespoon **soy sauce,** 1 teaspoon **ground ginger,** ½ teaspoon **dry mustard,** and **garlic salt** and **pepper** to taste.

Shrimp-stuffed Avocados

Creamy cool avocado halves, topped with shrimp and garnished with fresh asparagus spears, beets, and tomatoes, make an attractive spring luncheon salad. A tangy, creamy dressing complements it.

>   **Butter lettuce leaves**
>   **Tangy dressing (directions follow)**
>   3 **medium-size avocados**
>   **About 2 tablespoons lemon juice**
>   1 **to 1½ pounds small or medium-size
>   shrimp, cooked, shelled and deveined
>   (if needed), and chilled**
>   1 **pound cold cooked asparagus spears**
>   1 **small can (about 8 oz.) pickled beets,
>   drained**
>   1 **to 1½ dozen cherry tomatoes**

Arrange lettuce leaves on 6 salad plates or on 1 large tray. Prepare tangy dressing; set aside.

Peel, pit, and halve avocados; brush all over with lemon juice. Place ½ avocado on each plate. Fill each half with shrimp; surround filled avocado with asparagus, beets, and tomatoes. Pass dressing to spoon over individual servings. Makes 6 servings.

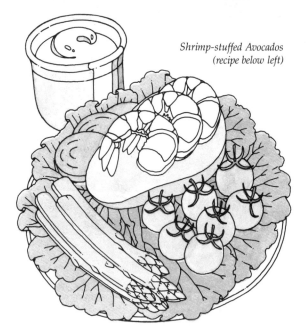

*Shrimp-stuffed Avocados
(recipe below left)*

Tangy dressing. In a blender, combine ½ cup **salad oil,** ¼ cup **tarragon vinegar,** 2 tablespoons **Dijon mustard,** 2 teaspoons **prepared horseradish,** 1 tablespoon **catsup,** ½ teaspoon **salt,** ¼ teaspoon **cayenne,** and 1 **hard-cooked egg** (cut up); whirl until smooth. Stir in ¼ cup *each* finely chopped **celery** and **green onion.**

Chilled Leeks & Shrimp

Elegant leeks match up with tiny pink shrimp for a first-course dinner idea.

>   6 **to 8 leeks, about 1 inch in diameter**
>   **Water**
> ¾ **cup mayonnaise**
> 1½ **tablespoons lemon juice**
>   3 **tablespoons Dijon mustard**
> ½ **cup whipping cream, whipped**
>   **Salt and pepper**
>   **Romaine leaves**
> ¾ **to 1 pound small cooked shrimp**

Cut leeks in half lengthwise. Trim off dark green tops, leaving 6 to 7 inches of white stem. Rinse leeks well and place in a large frying pan with enough water to cover. (If pan won't hold all the leeks at once, repeat process.) Cover and cook over medium heat for 5 to 7 minutes or just until tender when pierced. Drain, cover, and refrigerate until next day, if desired.

Combine mayonnaise, lemon juice, and mustard; fold in whipped cream and add salt and pepper to taste. Cover and chill.

Arrange romaine leaves on a serving platter or on 6 to 8 salad plates. Place 2 leek halves on each and evenly distribute shrimp over top. Pass mustard dressing to spoon over. Makes 6 to 8 servings.

Salad & Cheese—Natural Partners

A green salad served along with some special cheese may strike just the right dramatic note between a dinner entrée and dessert, or at the very end of a meal.

We offer here two excellent green salads—the one with shallots is robust, the other mild—and to go with them, we suggest some especially complementary cheeses.

Most of these cheeses, luxuriant and subtle in flavor, fall into the dessert or appetizer category. They range from the mildness of domestic cream cheese to the nippy quality of French goat cheese; from the mellowness of Sanglier, to the assertiveness of Camembert. They are richer and usually costlier than the more familiar cheeses, such as Swiss or Cheddars. Many of the imported, and some of the domestic varieties may be new to you, but discovering them in this context is fun and good eating. They're available in cheese specialty shops, gourmet food stores, and quite often in supermarkets.

To serve a salad and cheese course, first allow the cheese to mellow at room temperature for several hours; if the cheese is a ripened type, it should be fully ripe. Dish up the salad and pass the cheese; each person cuts off a portion and puts it on or alongside the salad. Allow at least 1 ounce of cheese per serving.

Cheeses to Serve with Salad

Boursault. Rich, smooth French cream cheese in a fat, round cake; slight, edible crust.

Boursin. Soft, rich French cheese, plain or with herbs; no crust; foil rectangles or round cakes.

Breakfast cheese. Domestic ripened semisoft cheese in small cake; edible crust.

Danish white soft ripened cheese or dessert cheese. Small rectangle; edible crust.

Gervais. Tangy French cream cheese, plain or with herbs; no crust; packaged in foil.

Le beau Pasteur. French process cheese in a wheel; packaged in foil, cut in wedges.

Pont L'Evèque. Rectangular semisoft French cheese; trim off rind.

Sanglier. Semisoft French cheese in a wheel; cut in wedges; trim off rind.

Sainte Maure pur Chèvre. Log-shaped French goat cheese; edible crust.

Brie. French, Danish, and domestic varieties of a soft ripened cheese that comes in small and large cakes, or cut in wedges; edible crust.

Camembert. French, Danish, and domestic soft ripened cheese that comes in small and large cakes, or cut in wedges; edible crust.

Mild Cheeses to Serve with Salad

Cherry cheese. French process, kirsch-flavored cheese in small or large cakes.

La Vache Qui Rit. The French process "laughing cow cheese;" small wedges or cubes; packaged in foil.

Shallot & Greens Salad

4 tablespoons minced fresh or freeze-dried shallots
6 tablespoons olive oil or salad oil
3 tablespoons red wine vinegar
1 tablespoon Dijon mustard
2 cups lightly packed watercress leaves (or 1 cup broken pieces of chicory)
2 medium-size heads butter lettuce, broken into bite-size pieces
Salt

Stir together shallots, oil, vinegar, and mustard. Combine watercress and lettuce in a salad bowl. Pour over the dressing and sprinkle with salt to taste; mix salad well. Makes 4 to 6 servings.

Three Greens Salad

1 large clove garlic, split
6 tablespoons olive oil or salad oil
2½ tablespoons red wine vinegar
2 cups *each* lightly packed bite-size pieces of butter lettuce, red leaf lettuce, and center leaves of romaine
Salt and freshly ground pepper

Combine garlic with oil and let stand for 30 minutes to 1 hour; discard garlic. Add vinegar to oil and stir to blend. Pour dressing over mixed greens; add salt and pepper to taste and mix well. Makes 4 to 6 servings.

Marinated Cucumbers with Shrimp

Cucumbers have a remarkably adaptable flavor. Teamed up with tiny shrimp, they take well to a soy-vinegar marinade. Salt cucumbers first to draw off excess moisture before adding dressing.

- 2 cucumbers, peeled and cut in ⅛-inch-thick slices
- 1 teaspoon *each* salt and sugar
- ¼ cup white wine vinegar or tarragon vinegar
- 1 tablespoon soy sauce
  Lettuce leaves
- ¼ pound small cooked shrimp or 1 can (4½ oz.) shrimp, drained
  Watercress sprigs (optional)

Mix cucumbers with salt and let stand for about 15 minutes; drain well and place in a bowl. Add sugar, vinegar, and soy sauce; cover and refrigerate for 1 to 4 hours.

Line a serving platter with lettuce leaves. Lift cucumbers from marinade (reserve marinade) and arrange in a large circle, overlapping slices. Mound shrimp in center of cucumbers. Drizzle 2 tablespoons marinade over shrimp. Garnish with watercress, if desired. Makes 4 to 6 servings.

Classic Crab Louis

Pictured on facing page

Which Louis originated this famous crab salad remains a point of debate; but Solari's Grill in San Francisco was among the first restaurants to serve it, around 1911.

- 1 cup mayonnaise
- ¼ cup tomato-based chili sauce
- ¼ cup *each* finely chopped green pepper and green onion
- ¼ cup whipping cream, whipped
  Salt
  Lemon juice
- 2 small heads iceberg lettuce
- 2 large Dungeness crabs, cooked, cracked, and shelled, or ¾ to 1 pound cooked or canned crab
- 4 large tomatoes, cut in wedges
- 4 hard-cooked eggs, cut in wedges
  Parsley sprigs
  Lemon wedges

FRESH DUNGENESS or other hard-shell crab is among the ingredients assembled for a classic crab Louis salad. Serve with a tangy mayonnaise dressing and sourdough French bread. The recipe is on this page.

Mix together mayonnaise, chili sauce, pepper, and onion; fold into whipped cream. Season with salt and lemon juice to taste.

Arrange outer leaves of lettuce on 4 large plates; shred remaining lettuce and divide evenly among 4 plates. Place crab (reserve legs) on shredded lettuce. Arrange tomatoes and eggs around crab.

Pour over dressing and garnish with crab legs, parsley, and lemon wedges. Makes 4 servings.

Mexican Crab Louis

Thousand island-style dressing is replaced with guacamole in a Mexican rendition of an old favorite, Crab Louis. You can use crab, shrimp, or a combination of both.

- 2 tablespoons wine vinegar
- 4 tablespoons olive oil or salad oil
  Salt
- 4 cups romaine, broken in pieces
- 1 pound cooked or canned crab or medium-size shrimp (cooked, shelled, and deveined)
- 1 cup homemade guacamole or other avocado dressing (page 92), or 1 can (6 oz.) frozen guacamole, thawed
- 2 or 3 hard-cooked eggs, sliced
- ⅓ cup sour cream
- 1 lime, cut in wedges

Combine vinegar and oil; add salt to taste. Place romaine pieces in a bowl; add oil-vinegar mixture and toss, coating leaves evenly. Arrange on a large platter or 4 individual salad plates. For 1 large salad, arrange a ring of crab or shrimp on greens, mounding guacamole in center. Garnish with eggs and mound sour cream onto guacamole. For individual salads, divide ingredients equally and arrange in the same manner. Garnish with lime wedges to squeeze over. Makes 4 servings.

Crab & Cucumber Salad

Croutons are mixed right in with this crab-vegetable salad. Don't let it stand around or you'll have soggy croutons. Top with avocado slices.

- 4 large cucumbers, peeled and sliced
- 1 medium-size onion, sliced and separated into rings
- 1 package (6 oz.) herb and cheese-seasoned croutons
- ½ pound cooked or canned crab
- 1 cup prepared salad dressing or mayonnaise
- ⅔ cup white wine vinegar
  Salt and pepper
- 1 avocado
- ½ teaspoon paprika

(Continued on next page)

In a salad bowl, mix together cucumber slices, onion rings, croutons, and crab. Combine salad dressing and vinegar; pour over cucumber mixture and add salt and pepper to taste. Peel, pit, and slice avocado. Arrange slices over top; then sprinkle with paprika. Makes 8 servings.

Lobster & Papaya Goddess Salad

Green goddess dressing is spooned over lobster and papaya to make an elegant salad for a special occasion. Look for rock lobster tails in the frozen food section of your supermarket. Plan on one lobster for two servings.

 1 frozen rock lobster tail (about ½ pound), thawed
 1 large papaya
   Romaine leaves
   Lime wedges
   Green goddess dressing, homemade (page 90) or purchased

Cook lobster tail following package directions; chill. Meanwhile, peel papaya, cut in half, and scoop out seeds. Arrange romaine leaves on 2 salad plates and place ½ papaya on each.

Remove chilled lobster meat from shell; cut in half lengthwise. Cut each half into ½-inch chunks and reassemble, laying one half of the lobster tail across each papaya half. Garnish with lime wedges. Serve green goddess dressing to spoon over. Makes 2 servings.

Curried Tuna Salad for Two

A spicy curry dressing tops an array of tuna, shell macaroni, apple, and almonds to be served from a salad bowl or on 2 lettuce-lined salad plates.

 ½ cup small shell macaroni
 1 large apple
 2½ tablespoons lemon juice
 1 cup sliced celery
 ½ cup raisins (or halved seedless grapes)
 ¼ cup thinly sliced green onion
 1 can (about 7 oz.) tuna, drained
 ½ cup mayonnaise
 1 teaspoon Dijon mustard
 1½ teaspoons curry powder
   Salt
 ⅓ cup sliced almonds
   Lettuce leaves

Cook macaroni as directed on package; drain and chill. Dice apple; in a salad bowl, mix apple with

lemon juice until coated. Add celery, raisins, onion, and macaroni. Add tuna, broken in chunks.

Combine mayonnaise, mustard, and curry powder. Mix gently into salad. Add salt to taste. Cover and chill up to 2 hours. Mix half the almonds into salad. Serve in the salad bowl or on 2 lettuce-lined plates. Sprinkle top with remaining almonds. Makes 2 servings.

Caper-Tuna Salad

Seedless grapes and capers distinguish this refreshing main-dish tuna salad surrounded by sliced fruits of your choice.

 3 cans (about 7 oz. *each*) tuna, drained
 2 cups seedless grapes
 2 cups thinly sliced celery
 1 jar (about 2 oz.) capers, well drained
 ¼ cup sliced green onion
 ½ cup *each* mayonnaise and sour cream
 1 tablespoon lemon juice
 1 teaspoon Dijon mustard
   Salt and pepper
   Lettuce leaves
   Fresh fruits (suggestions follow)

In a large bowl, mix together tuna, grapes, celery, capers, and onion. In a small bowl or jar, combine mayonnaise, sour cream, lemon juice, and mustard; add salt and pepper to taste and blend well. Cover and refrigerate salad and dressing separately for at least 2 hours.

To serve, line a large, shallow salad bowl with lettuce leaves. Toss tuna mixture with dressing, mound on top of lettuce, and surround with fruit. Makes about 8 servings.

Fresh fruits. Choose 2 or more of the following fruits: cantaloupe, honeydew melon, peaches, pears, plums, or apricots. They should be well chilled, peeled (if desired), and sliced.

Tuna with Bean Sprouts

Lively, crunchy textures are added whenever bean sprouts join a salad. This mixture can double as a sandwich filling on pumpernickel bread.

 1 can (about 7 oz.) tuna, drained
 ¾ cup fresh bean sprouts
 3 teaspoons capers, drained
 ¼ cup mayonnaise
 1 teaspoon soy sauce
   Lettuce leaves
 2 whole sweet midget pickles
 2 whole sweet cherry peppers

Mix together tuna, sprouts, capers, mayonnaise, and soy.

To serve, line two salad plates with lettuce. Mound tuna mixture equally onto each plate. Slice pickles lengthwise, almost to one end, (about 4 slices in each); fan slices out. Place on tuna and garnish with peppers. Makes 2 salads.

Tuna-Avocado Tomato Stacks

Little tomato towers are impressive presentations filled with a zippy tuna-avocado mixture. The tomatoes are sliced then reassembled to show off ribbons of filling.

1 medium-size avocado
2 tablespoons lemon juice
1 large clove garlic, minced or pressed
⅓ cup coarsely chopped celery or green pepper
2 green onions, thinly sliced
1 can (about 7 oz.) tuna, drained
   Salt, pepper, and liquid hot pepper seasoning
4 medium-to-large tomatoes
   Lettuce leaves

Peel and pit avocado; mash coarsely in a bowl. Blend in lemon juice, garlic, celery, and onion. Break tuna into chunks and gently stir into avocado mixture. Add salt, pepper, and hot pepper seasoning to taste. Cover and refrigerate until next day, if desired.

Peel tomatoes and cut out stems. Cut each tomato into 4 thick slices. Spread tuna-avocado mixture between slices, stacking each tomato on a lettuce-lined plate. Cover and refrigerate up to 4 hours, if desired. Makes 4 servings.

Tuna-Avocado Tomato Stacks
(recipe above)

Tuna Salad with Fruit

Juicy orange sections and seedless grapes make a refreshing garnish for this tuna luncheon salad sprinkled with toasted almonds.

2 medium-size oranges
¼ cup *each* mayonnaise and sour cream
   Dash of liquid hot pepper seasoning
2 cans (about 7 oz. *each*) tuna, drained
1 cup thinly sliced celery
   Salt and pepper
¼ cup slivered almonds
   Lettuce leaves
1 cup seedless grapes, halved

Grate 1 teaspoon orange peel from 1 orange; set peel aside. Then peel oranges, removing white membrane, and lift out orange sections. Cover and chill.

Combine grated orange peel, mayonnaise, sour cream, and hot pepper seasoning; blend well. In a large bowl, break tuna apart into large chunks; add celery and sour cream dressing, then toss gently. Season with salt and pepper to taste. Cover and refrigerate for 2 to 4 hours.

Spread almonds in a shallow pan and toast in a 350° oven for about 8 minutes or until golden.

To serve, line a serving platter or four salad plates with lettuce leaves. Mound tuna mixture in center; sprinkle top generously with almonds. Arrange orange sections and grapes around tuna. Makes 4 servings.

Chili-flavored Beef & Corn Salad

Cold leftovers from a roast or barbecue turn a salad into a whole meal. This beef salad is boldly seasoned with chili powder, bits of hot pepper, and fresh coriander or parsley.

   Chili dressing (directions follow)
2 cups cold cooked beef, cut in matchstick-size pieces
3 cups shredded cabbage
1 medium-size green pepper, cut in short thin slivers
2 small tomatoes, diced
1 small red onion, sliced and separated into rings
1 can (about 17 oz.) whole kernel corn, drained, or 1 can (12 oz.) whole kernel corn with sweet peppers, drained
¼ cup chopped fresh coriander (cilantro)
2 hard-cooked eggs, cut in wedges
   Sprigs of fresh coriander (cilantro) or parsley (optional)

(Continued on next page)

...Chili-flavored Beef & Corn Salad (cont'd.)

Prepare chili dressing and combine with beef; cover and refrigerate for 30 minutes to 1 hour.

Add cabbage, pepper, tomatoes, onion, corn, and chopped coriander to meat mixture; toss together to mix. Garnish with eggs and coriander sprigs, if desired. Makes 4 servings.

Chili dressing. Stir together ½ cup **salad oil,** ⅓ cup **red wine vinegar,** 1 teaspoon **chili powder,** 1½ teaspoons **garlic salt,** ¼ to ½ teaspoon **crushed red pepper.**

Taco Salad

Pictured on facing page

Mexican flavors of chili and cumin permeate this spicy beef and beans whole-meal salad.

    1 pound lean ground beef
    1 medium-size onion, chopped
    1 can (15 oz.) kidney beans, drained
 1½ teaspoons chili powder
    ½ teaspoon ground cumin
    ½ cup catsup or tomato sauce
    2 medium-size avocados
    1 medium-size head iceberg lettuce,
        shredded
    1 cup (4 oz.) shredded Cheddar or
        jack cheese
    2 medium-size tomatoes, cut in wedges
    3 hard-cooked eggs, cut in wedges
        Tortilla chips
        Sour cream
        Red onion rings
        Sliced ripe olives
        Chopped green onion
        Green peperoncini (optional)

In a wide frying pan over medium-high heat, crumble in beef and cook with onion until meat has lost its pink color and onion is limp; drain and discard drippings. Stir in kidney beans, chili powder, cumin, and catsup; simmer over low heat for about 5 minutes.

Peel, pit, and slice avocados. Arrange lettuce on 4 dinner plates. Top with equal amounts of beef mixture, cheese, tomato and egg wedges, avocado slices and tortilla chips. Top with dollops of sour cream, onion rings, olives, and a sprinkling of green onion. Garnish with green peperoncini, if desired. Makes 4 servings.

Mexican Beef & Beans in Lettuce Wraps

Cool, crisp lettuce leaves make refreshing low-calorie wraps in place of tortillas for a hot meat-and-vegetable mixture to eat out of hand like tacos.

    ¾ pound *each* chorizo sausage and lean
        ground beef
    1 large onion, chopped
    2 cloves garlic, minced or pressed
 1½ teaspoons chili powder
    ½ teaspoon ground cumin
    ¼ teaspoon cayenne
    1 can (17 oz.) refried beans
    1 can (2¼ oz.) sliced ripe olives, drained
    1 can (4 oz.) diced green chiles
    2 cups (8 oz.) shredded Cheddar cheese
        Salt and pepper
    ½ cup sour cream
    3 tablespoons *each* thinly sliced radishes
        and green onion
    2 large heads butter lettuce

Crumble sausage and beef in a large frying pan and cook over medium heat, stirring occasionally, until meat is lightly browned. Remove meat and discard all but 2 tablespoons drippings. Add onion, garlic, chili powder, cumin, and cayenne; continue cooking, stirring, until onion is limp.

Stir in refried beans, olives, and chiles; reduce heat to low and cook, stirring, until bubbly and hot. Stir in 1 cup of the cheese and salt and pepper to taste. Turn into a shallow 1½-quart baking dish. Sprinkle remaining 1 cup cheese over top.

Broil about 6 inches from heat just until cheese melts (about 3 minutes). Mound sour cream in center; sprinkle with radishes and green onion. Spoon mixture into lettuce leaves, roll up, and eat out of hand. Makes 6 servings.

Sesame Ham & Won Ton Salad

Toasted sesame seed gives this green salad a nutty flavor. Crisp, crunchy strips of fried won ton skins add an interesting texture. Look for won ton wrappers in the refrigerator or freezer section of your market or check Oriental grocery stores.

    2 dozen won ton skins
        Salad oil
    1 bunch watercress (about ¼ lb.)
    6 cups shredded iceberg lettuce
    1 can (8 oz.) water chestnuts, drained
        and sliced
    2 cups cold cooked ham cut in julienne
        strips, or 2 cups cold cooked shredded
        chicken or turkey
        Sesame dressing (directions follow)

(Continued on page 49)

TOWERING TACO SALADS offer a mingling of hot and cold, both in spices and temperature. Hot beef with beans is mounded on chilled shredded lettuce, then piled high with tempting garnishes. The recipe is on this page.

48.

A leisurely way to entertain guests, especially in warm weather, is to plan a salad-sandwich party. It's an idea adapted from the delicatessen-type sandwich shops of Europe.

Like sandwich shop customers, party guests choose from a collection of boldly flavorful salad-type sandwich fillings. Here we offer a protein-rich filling (chicken) and three vegetable salads (celery root, mushroom, and ratatouille). All can be made at least a day in advance.

This party can serve any number of guests. For a group of six serve all four salads along with about ¾ pound thinly sliced ham. You could easily multiply these quantities for a larger group and offer thinly sliced Swiss cheese as well.

For a group of four, you might serve chicken salad accompanied by one or two of the vegetable salads, or serve all three vegetable salads with ham or cheese.

For bread, buy baguettes (long, skinny loaves of French bread), regular long loaves of French bread, or French rolls. (A 1-pound loaf makes six to eight servings.) Split bread lengthwise and butter the halves. Place on cutting board or in a basket.

You'll also need a medium-size head of romaine, red leaf, or iceberg lettuce, or two small heads of butter lettuce for every three or four servings.

Accompany the meal with white wine, iced tea, or beer. For dessert you might offer wedges of cantaloupe or honeydew.

Ratatouille Salad

In a wide frying pan over medium-high heat, cook, stirring, 1 medium-size **onion** (finely chopped) and 1 **clove garlic** (minced or pressed) in 3 tablespoons **olive oil** or salad oil until limp. Add 1 small (about ¾ lb.) **eggplant** (cut into 1-inch cubes), 1 medium-size **zucchini** (cut into ½-inch-thick slices), 1 medium-size **green pepper** (cut into ¼-inch strips), ¼ cup chopped **parsley,** 1 teaspoon *each* **dry basil** and **salt,** and 1 can (1 lb.) **Italian-style tomatoes** (including liquid); break tomatoes into small pieces with spoon.

Cover and simmer, stirring occasionally, until all vegetables are tender (about 25 minutes). Cook, uncovered, stirring occasionally, over high heat until most of the liquid has evaporated. Cool, cover, and chill if made ahead. Serve with about ⅓ cup grated **Parmesan cheese** to sprinkle over individual servings. Makes 4 cups.

Marinated Mushroom Salad

Wash and trim ends from 1¼ pounds small **mushrooms** (or cut medium-size mushrooms in quarters). Place in boiling **salted water** to cover; reduce heat and simmer, uncovered, for 5 minutes; drain and let cool.

Mix together 6 tablespoons **olive oil;** 2 tablespoons **lemon juice;** 1 clove **garlic** (minced or pressed); ½ teaspoon *each* crushed **whole black pepper, coriander seed,** and **mustard seed;** and ½ teaspoon **salt.** Add mushrooms, 1 small **onion** (finely chopped), and ½ cup chopped **parsley;** stir to blend. Cover and chill, stirring occasionally, for at least 2 hours. Makes 3½ cups.

Celery Root Salad

Combine 6 tablespoons **olive oil** or salad oil, 3 tablespoons **white wine vinegar,** 1 teaspoon *each* **salt, sugar,** and **caraway seed,** and 1 clove **garlic** (minced or pressed).

Cut off tops from 1¼ pounds (about 2 medium-size) **celery root** (or 4 medium-size turnips) and peel; wash well. Cut in matchstick-size pieces (you should have about 3½ cups). Stir into oil mixture. Cover and chill, stirring occasionally, for at least 2 hours.

Just before serving, pour salad through colander to drain off excess marinade. Mix celery root with ¼ cup **mayonnaise.** Makes 3 cups.

Curried Chicken Salad

Stir together ½ cup **mayonnaise,** ½ teaspoon **garlic salt,** 1 teaspoon **curry powder,** ⅛ teaspoon **cayenne,** ½ teaspoon **prepared mustard,** 2 teaspoons **lemon juice,** and 2 tablespoons finely chopped **Major Grey's chutney.** Add 3½ cups cold **cooked chicken** (cut into ½-inch chunks), ⅔ cup thinly sliced **celery,** 2 thinly sliced **green onions,** and 1 small **apple** (diced); stir to blend. Cover and chill if made ahead. Just before serving, sprinkle top with 3 tablespoons toasted **sliced almonds.** Makes 4½ cups.

...*Sesame Ham & Won Ton Salad (cont'd.)*

Cut won tons into ½-inch strips. In a frying pan, heat about ¼ inch salad oil over medium heat. Add won ton strips, a few at a time, and fry until crisp and golden (about 30 seconds). With a slotted spoon, remove from pan, drain, and let cool (store airtight at room temperature, if made a day ahead).

Pluck off and discard watercress stems. In a salad bowl, combine watercress leaves, shredded lettuce, water chestnuts, and ham. Cover and chill, if made ahead.

To serve, add fried won ton strips to salad. Prepare sesame dressing, pour over salad, and toss to coat. Makes about 4 servings.

Sesame dressing. In a small frying pan, combine ¼ cup **salad oil** and 2 tablespoons **sesame seed;** cook over medium-low heat, stirring occasionally, until seeds are golden (about 2 minutes). Let cool. Stir in 2½ tablespoons *each* **soy sauce** and **white wine vinegar,** 1½ tablespoons **sugar,** and ¼ teaspoon **salt.**

Thai Pineapple-Pork Salad

Well-seasoned pork is placed on chilled sweet pineapple rings and surrounded by crisp mild greens to accentuate the differences of hot and cold, sweet and savory. Serve as a light luncheon entrée with hot crusty rolls and butter.

        Butter lettuce leaves
    1   medium-size pineapple (about 3½ lbs.),
            peeled, cored, and cut into 4 rounds,
            each about 1 inch thick
    1   pound lean ground pork
    1   small onion, finely chopped
        Lime dressing (directions follow)
    6   tablespoons finely chopped, salted
            roasted peanuts
    4   to 8 pickled red chiles or sweet cherry
            peppers
        Sprigs of fresh coriander (cilantro) or mint

Line 4 individual salad plates with lettuce leaves. Lay a pineapple slice on each plate; cover and chill.

In a large frying pan, cook pork over medium heat, stirring to break up, until it loses its pinkness (about 5 minutes). Add onion and cook, stirring, until limp. Skim off and discard any fat. Prepare lime dressing, add to meat, and cook, stirring, until boiling and slightly thickened (about 30 seconds). Mound equal portions of the hot pork mixture onto each pineapple slice; sprinkle peanuts over pork. Garnish each plate with 1 or 2 peppers and sprigs of coriander. Serve immediately. Makes 4 servings.

Lime dressing. Stir together ½ teaspoon **cornstarch,** 2 tablespoons **sugar,** ⅛ teaspoon **cayenne,** ½ teaspoon **salt,** 1 teaspoon grated **lime peel,** 3 tablespoons **lime juice,** and 1 tablespoon **soy sauce.**

Cheese & Wurst Salad

The German word for sausage is wurst. One popular German-style sausage, knackwurst, is widely available in American markets. If you can't find it, substitute an equal weight of regular or garlic frankfurters.

    4   large knackwurst (about 1¼ lbs.)
        Water
    ¼   pound Swiss cheese
    ½   cup *each* thinly sliced celery, diced sweet
            pickle, and diced green pepper
    2   small red onions, thinly sliced and
            separated into rings
    2   hard-cooked eggs, sliced
        Mustard dressing (directions follow)

Place wurst in a pan with enough water to cover; bring to a boil, reduce heat, and simmer for 10 minutes. Remove sausage from water and set aside to cool.

Peel and discard casings, if desired. Slice meat and cheese into julienne strips about 3 inches long. Combine celery, pickle, and green pepper. Place wurst, cheese, celery mixture, onion rings, and egg slices in a salad bowl. Cover and chill, if made ahead. Prepare mustard dressing. To serve, mix dressing evenly into salad. Makes 4 to 6 servings.

Mustard dressing. Combine ½ cup *each* **sour cream** and **mayonnaise,** 3 tablespoons **prepared hot German mustard** or Dijon mustard, and 1 tablespoon *each* **prepared horseradish** and **cider vinegar;** stir until blended.

Sauerkraut & Wurst Salad

Hearty sauerkraut with sausage makes a delightful German dish to be served with dark bread and thick soup for a hearty whole meal.

    3   large knackwurst (about 1 lb.)
    2   medium-size tart apples
    3   tablespoons lemon juice
    1   can (1 lb.) sauerkraut, rinsed and drained
    ½   cup diced dill pickle
    1   small red onion, chopped
    ¼   teaspoon dill weed
    1   teaspoon caraway seed
    ½   teaspoon salt
    3   tablespoons *each* sugar and salad oil

Place wurst in a pan with enough water to cover; bring to a boil, reduce heat, and simmer for 10 minutes. Remove from water and set aside to cool.

Peel and dice apples into a salad bowl; pour over lemon juice and toss. Peel and discard casings from wurst, if desired; cut meat into ¼-inch-thick slices.

(Continued on page 51)

... *Sauerkraut & Wurst Salad (cont'd.)*

Add wurst, sauerkraut, pickle, onion, dill, and caraway seed to apples. Combine salt, sugar, and oil; mix into salad and chill for several hours. Makes 4 servings.

Hot Potato Wurst Salad

Pictured on facing page

Knackwurst and bratwurst slices make this hot potato salad a meal with the addition of rye bread, spicy mustard, and a stout beer.

    6 to 8 medium-size thin-skinned potatoes
        (about 2½ lbs.)
        Boiling water
    1 tablespoon salad oil
    2 *each* large knackwurst (about 10 oz.) and
        large bratwurst (about 12 oz.), casings
        removed and meat cut into ¼-inch
        slanting slices
    4 teaspoons *each* all-purpose flour and sugar
    1 teaspoon *each* salt, dry mustard, and
        celery seed
    ⅔ cup regular-strength chicken broth
    ⅓ cup white wine vinegar
    ¼ cup finely chopped parsley
    1 small red onion, sliced and separated
        into rings
    ½ cup sliced celery

Place potatoes in 1 inch of boiling water; cover and cook just until tender when pierced (about 30 minutes); drain. When cool enough to handle, peel and slice potatoes; set aside.

In a wide frying pan over medium heat, add oil and wurst and cook, stirring, until lightly browned; remove wurst from pan and set aside. To pan add flour, sugar, salt, mustard, and celery seed. Cook, stirring, until mixture is hot and bubbly. Gradually stir in broth and vinegar; cook, stirring, until dressing boils and thickens.

Gently stir potatoes, wurst, parsley, onion, and celery into dressing until coated and hot throughout. Makes 6 servings.

Meat Salad

You can use cold cooked beef, ham, chicken, or turkey as the base for this nourishing salad that can double as a sandwich filler for Arab pocket bread.

HOT POTATO WURST SALAD is a zestful change from traditional picnic potato salad. Accompanied with dark brown bread and a spicy mustard, this high-protein salad serves as a whole meal. The recipe is on this page.

    1 cup chopped cold cooked beef, ham,
        or chicken
    ¾ cup shredded carrot or cabbage
    ½ cup (2 oz.) shredded Swiss cheese
    2 tablespoons sliced green onion
    5 tablespoons mayonnaise or salad dressing
    1 tablespoon sweet pickle relish
    ¼ teaspoon *each* prepared mustard and
        prepared horseradish
        Salt and pepper
        Lettuce leaves

In a bowl, mix together beef, carrot, cheese, and onion. In a separate bowl or jar, combine mayonnaise, pickle relish, mustard, and horseradish. Stir dressing into meat mixture until well blended, then season to taste with salt and pepper. Cover and refrigerate for several hours to blend flavors.

To serve, arrange lettuce leaves on 4 salad plates and spoon equal portions of salad onto each. Makes 4 servings.

Lemon Beef Salad

The refreshing mix of thinly sliced beef and vegetables is hearty enough for a light lunch or supper accompanied by crusty rolls or breadsticks.

Most of this salad can be made in advance. While the meat marinates, you can cut and prepare the remaining ingredients.

    1 *each* medium-size cucumber and
        small onion
    1 teaspoon salt
    2 large lemons
    1 teaspoon sugar
    ½ pound thinly sliced cold cooked beef,
        cut into strips about ¾ by 2 inches
        (about 1½ cups)
    1 cup *each* shredded carrots and thinly
        sliced celery
    ½ cup chopped salted roasted peanuts

Peel cucumber, if desired. Cut it in half lengthwise, then in thin crosswise slices. Cut and slice onion the same way. Combine cucumber, onion, and salt; cover and chill for 30 minutes to 1 hour. Drain thoroughly and discard liquid.

With a vegetable peeler, remove all of the thin yellow outer peel from one of the lemons. Cut peel into thin 1-inch-long slivers. Juice the lemon (you should have about 3 tablespoons). Mix together the 3 tablespoons lemon juice, sugar, and peel. Pour over drained cucumber and onion; add beef and mix together. Cover and chill for 1 to 4 hours, stirring occasionally.

To serve, mix carrots, celery, and peanuts with beef mixture. Mound salad on 2 salad plates. Cut remaining lemon in half lengthwise, then in thin crosswise slices. Arrange a border of lemon slices around each salad. Makes 2 servings.

Rice & Pasta Salads

Creamy and satisfying, these salads are at their best
when the flavors have time to blend.
They are sturdy and portable candidates
for picnics and potlucks.

Minted Rice-stuffed Tomatoes

Big beautiful tomatoes, when hollowed out,
make ideal containers for many stuffings. Mint
and curry-flavored rice salad is an excellent choice
and a good accompaniment for barbecued meats,
oven roasts, or assorted cold cuts.

     6 **large tomatoes**
     2 **cups cold cooked rice**
     ½ **cup raisins**
     2 **tablespoons** *each* **chopped green pepper,
         green onion, parsley, and fresh mint
          (or 1 tablespoon dry mint)**
        Oil and lemon dressing (directions follow)
        Salt and pepper
        Mint sprigs
        About 1 cup unflavored yogurt

Peel tomatoes, if desired, and remove stems. Cut a
thin slice from the top of each tomato, chop, and
set aside. Scoop out pulp and seeds (reserve for
other uses); invert shells to drain.

In a bowl, mix together chopped tomato, rice,
raisins, green pepper, onion, parsley, and mint.
Prepare the oil and lemon dressing; stir into rice
mixture until thoroughly blended. Season to taste
with salt and pepper.

Fill tomato shells with equal portions of rice mixture; cover and chill if made ahead. To serve, garnish with mint sprigs; pass yogurt to spoon over.
Makes 6 servings.

Oil and lemon dressing. In a small bowl, combine
¼ cup **salad oil,** 2 tablespoons *each* **lemon juice**
and **sweet pickle relish,** 1 tablespoon **catsup,** ½
teaspoon *each* **dry mustard** and **chili powder,** and 1
teaspoon **curry powder.**

Rice Salad with Pesto Dressing

Pungent basil leaves mixed with Parmesan cheese
and olive oil make a flavor impact on this cooling
rice salad.

1 tablespoon dry basil
¼ cup shredded or grated Parmesan cheese
3 tablespoons lemon juice
½ cup olive oil or salad oil
¼ pound mushrooms, thinly sliced
1 jar (2 oz.) sliced pimentos, drained
4 cups cold cooked rice
1 green pepper, seeded and diced
1 canned green chile, seeded and
   finely chopped
  Salt
  Romaine leaves
  Green pepper rings

In a blender, combine basil, cheese, and lemon juice. With blender whirling on lowest speed, slowly pour in oil to make a creamy-smooth mixture.

Place mushrooms in a bowl. Coarsely chop pimento (reserve a few strips for garnish); add to mushrooms with rice, green pepper, and chile. Pour over dressing, toss gently; add salt to taste. Cover and chill.

To serve, spoon salad into bowl lined with romaine leaves. Garnish with green pepper rings and pimento strips. Makes about 6 servings.

Zucchini-Rice Salad

A hearty salad of rice, zucchini, and eggplant can be the focus of a meal. Make the salad ahead, then serve with grilled sausage or barbecued chicken.

½ cup olive oil or salad oil
1 clove garlic, minced or pressed
1 small (about 1 lb.) eggplant, diced
½ pound zucchini, cut in ¼-inch-thick slices
1 small can (8 oz.) stewed tomatoes
¼ teaspoon *each* oregano and thyme leaves
1 cup short grain rice (such as
   California pearl)
2 cups regular-strength chicken broth
1 green pepper, seeded and diced
1 medium-size red onion, finely chopped
3 tablespoons lemon juice
  Salt and pepper
  Red lettuce leaves
2 medium-size tomatoes, cut in wedges

In a large frying pan, heat 4 tablespoons of the oil over medium-high heat; add garlic and eggplant and cook, stirring gently, until eggplant turns dark and softens (about 5 minutes). Add zucchini, stewed tomatoes, oregano, and thyme; cover and cook for about 2 minutes, shaking pan occasionally, until zucchini is tender-crisp. Remove lid and cook, stirring, until any excess liquid is evaporated. Transfer vegetable mixture to a bowl and cool.

To frying pan, add the remaining 4 tablespoons oil along with rice. Reduce heat to medium and cook, stirring, until rice turns opaque (about 5 minutes). Gradually stir in broth. Cover, reduce heat, and simmer until rice is tender (about 15 minutes); cool.

Just before serving, gently mix together vegetable mixture, rice, green pepper, onion, lemon juice, and salt and pepper to taste. Line a wide shallow bowl with lettuce leaves, then mound salad on lettuce. Garnish with tomato wedges. Makes 6 servings.

Thyme Rice Salad

Thyme is the predominant seasoning in this salad, yet the overall effect is surprisingly subtle and refreshing.

½ cup golden raisins
  Boiling water
3 cups cold cooked rice
6 tablespoons olive oil or salad oil
2 tablespoons cider vinegar
2 teaspoons thyme leaves
1 medium-size red apple
1 tablespoon lemon juice
¾ cup chopped pitted ripe olives
  Salt
1 cup (4 to 5 oz.) diced Gruyère or
   Samsoe cheese
  Lettuce leaves

Place raisins in a bowl. Pour water over raisins and let stand for 5 minutes; drain well. Add rice, oil, vinegar, and thyme. Core apple and finely chop. Mix apple with lemon juice; then stir apple and olives into salad. Season to taste with salt. Cover and chill.

Just before serving, stir in cheese; then spoon salad into a bowl lined with lettuce leaves. Makes about 6 servings.

Artichoke Rice Salad

The spicy marinade from canned marinated artichokes doubles as the dressing in this chilled rice salad.

1 jar (6 oz.) marinated artichoke hearts
¼ pound small mushrooms
2 medium-size ripe tomatoes, peeled,
   seeded and diced
1 cup medium-size pitted ripe olives
3 cups cold cooked rice
  Salt and pepper

Drain marinade from artichokes into frying pan; chop artichokes and set aside. Add mushrooms to marinade, cover, and cook over low heat for 10 minutes or until mushrooms are tender; remove from heat and cool.

In a bowl, mix together artichoke hearts, mushrooms and marinade, tomatoes, olives, and rice. Cover and chill for at least 4 hours. Add salt and pepper to taste. Makes about 6 servings.

Brown Rice Salad with Dates

Dates, cinnamon, and fresh orange slices lend a pleasant subtlety to brown rice salad.

- 1½ cups quick-cooking brown rice
- 7 tablespoons lemon juice
- ½ cup olive oil or salad oil
- ¼ teaspoon ground cinnamon
- ½ cup *each* minced parsley and fresh mint
- ¼ cup minced green onion
  About ⅔ cup pitted dates
- 3 large oranges
  Mint leaves or parsley sprigs

Cook rice according to package directions. In a bowl, mix together rice, lemon juice, olive oil, cinnamon, parsley, mint, and onion. Finely chop ⅓ cup of the dates and stir into rice; add salt to taste. Cover and chill.

Mound rice into shallow serving dish. Remove peel and white membrane from oranges; cut oranges crosswise into slices. Decorate salad with orange slices, remaining whole dates, and mint leaves. Makes 4 to 6 servings.

Curried Rice Salad Tray

Pack rice salad speckled with green peas into a bowl to mold shape. Unmold and serve with egg and tomato wedges and cold sliced meats.

- 6 cups cold cooked rice
- 1 package (10 oz.) frozen peas, thawed
- 1 cup thinly sliced celery
- ⅔ cup chopped green pepper
- 1 cup chopped green onion
- 1 cup sour cream
- 1 cup unflavored yogurt
- ½ cup Major Grey's chutney
- ½ teaspoon salt
- ½ to 1 teaspoon curry powder
  About 2 pounds cold sliced meat
- 4 large tomatoes, cut in wedges
- 6 to 8 hard-cooked eggs, quartered

In a large bowl, mix together rice, peas, celery, green pepper, and onion. In a blender combine sour cream, yogurt, chutney, salt, and curry powder; whirl until smooth. Add just enough dressing to rice mixture to moisten and hold ingredients together; toss gently. Pack rice into a 3-quart bowl, cover, and chill for at least 1 hour. Just before serving, invert bowl onto a large serving platter to unmold salad.

Arrange cold sliced meats, tomatoes, and hard-cooked eggs around rice salad. Pass remaining dressing to serve over individual portions. Makes about 12 servings.

Curried Egg & Rice Salad

Pictured on facing page

Hard-cooked egg halves are stuffed with chutney, then served on a bed of rice mixed with raisins and apricots.

- 6 hard-cooked eggs
- 2 tablespoons finely chopped Major Grey's chutney
- 4 teaspoons milk or half-and-half (light cream)
  Salt and pepper
- 3 tablespoons slivered almonds
- 3 cups *each* broken lettuce leaves and cold cooked rice
- 2 tablespoons *each* olive oil or salad oil and lemon juice
- 3 tablespoons *each* raisins and chopped dried apricots
- 3 tablespoons sliced green onion
  Curry dressing (directions follow)

Cut eggs in half lengthwise; scoop out yolks, mash well, and mix with chutney, milk, and salt and pepper to taste. Spoon mixture into egg white halves; chill if made ahead.

Spread almonds in a shallow pan and toast in a 350° oven until golden (about 8 minutes).

Arrange lettuce in a shallow salad bowl. Mix together rice, oil, lemon juice, raisins, apricots, and almonds. Mound on greens; arrange egg halves on rice and sprinkle with onion.

Prepare dressing and pass to spoon over servings. (Or prepare salad in individual servings of salad with egg halves, as shown in photograph on facing page.) Makes 6 servings.

Curry dressing. Mix 1 cup **unflavored yogurt,** ¼ cup **sour cream,** 3 tablespoons minced **green onion,** 1 small clove **garlic** (minced or pressed), 2 teaspoons **curry powder,** and ¼ teaspoon *each* **ground ginger** and **dry mustard.**

CHUTNEY-STUFFED CURRIED EGG HALVES garnish a salad of cold rice studded with raisins, chopped apricots, and toasted almonds. The recipe is on this page.

Crab-Rice Salad

Mixing cold cooked rice with crab meat conveys the impression of a lavish use of crab in this main-dish salad.

    Creamy dressing (directions follow)
2¼ cups cold cooked long grain rice
 ½ cup thinly sliced green onion
 1 large tomato, peeled, seeded, and diced
 1 cup thinly sliced celery
 ½ pound cold cooked or canned crab
    Salt and pepper
    Lettuce leaves
 2 hard-cooked eggs, sliced

Prepare creamy dressing. Combine rice, onion, tomato, celery, and dressing. Gently mix in crab and season to taste with salt and pepper. Cover and chill.

To serve, line a shallow salad bowl with lettuce leaves. Mound salad mixture on top and garnish with sliced eggs. Makes 4 servings.

Creamy dressing. Combine ⅓ cup *each* **mayonnaise** and **sour cream**, ¼ cup **tomato-based chili sauce**, 1 tablespoon **lemon juice**, and ½ teaspoon *each* **prepared mustard** and **prepared horseradish.**

Minted Rice-Tuna Salad

Fresh mint and lime give a refreshing flavor to this tuna and rice-based salad.

 ½ teaspoon grated lime peel
 3 tablespoons lime juice
 2 tablespoons chopped fresh mint or
    1 tablespoon dry mint
 2 cans (about 7 oz. *each*) tuna, drained
1½ cups cold cooked rice
 1 cup *each* thinly sliced celery and frozen
    peas, thawed
 2 tablespoons *each* chopped green onion
    and parsley
    Tangy dressing (directions follow)
    Salt and pepper
    Lettuce leaves
    Mint sprigs

Combine lime peel, juice, and mint leaves; set aside. In a bowl, mix together tuna, rice, celery, peas, onion, and parsley. Add lime-mint mixture and stir well. Cover and refrigerate for 2 to 4 hours. Prepare dressing, cover, and chill.

To serve, pour dressing over tuna mixture and toss gently. Season to taste with salt and pepper. Turn into a lettuce-lined bowl and garnish with mint sprigs. Makes 6 servings.

Tangy dressing. Combine 1 teaspoon **Dijon mustard**, 2 teaspoons **sugar**, and ½ teaspoon **liquid hot pepper seasoning.** Gradually add ½ cup **mayonnaise** and ¼ cup **buttermilk.** Blend well and chill.

Zarzuela

Make this hot Mexican fish and rice salad the center of attention for a buffet for 12 guests. It's a salad-casserole main dish that goes together in a smooth sequence of steps. Have all ingredients ready, then cook just before guests are due. You may hold the dish at serving temperature for as long as 2 hours on an electric warming tray, if desired, but zarzuela is best if not reheated.

 6 tablespoons olive oil or salad oil
 3 large onions, finely chopped
 1 cup minced parsley
 2 cups long grain rice
 1 can (1 lb. 12 oz.) whole tomatoes
 2 cans (8 oz. *each*) minced clams
 2 bottles (8 oz. *each*) clam juice
 2 cups water
 ¼ cup chopped fresh coriander
    (or 1 tablespoon dry cilantro leaves)
 2 to 2½ pounds boneless, skinned fish such
    as Greenland turbot, halibut, lingcod,
    or sea bass, cut in 1½-inch chunks
 ½ pound scallops, cut in ½-inch chunks
    Salt and pepper
    Accompaniments (suggestions follow)

Heat oil in a large pan (at least 5-qt. size) over medium-high heat; add onion and cook, stirring, until onion is limp. Stir in parsley and rice and continue to cook, stirring, until some of the rice is lightly toasted.

Stir in tomatoes and their juice (break up tomatoes with a spoon). Also stir in clams and their liquid, clam juice, water, and coriander. Raise heat and bring to a boil, then cover; reduce heat, and simmer for 15 minutes.

Add fish chunks and scallops to rice and press them down into rice; continue to cook on low heat, stirring occasionally for about 10 minutes or until fish flakes readily when prodded with a fork. Season to taste with salt and pepper.

(Continued on page 59)

Artichokes...Attractive Serving Containers for Salads

Large whole artichokes make attractive serving containers for flavorful salads. And you can use the extra dressing as a dipping sauce for the leaves and the tasty heart.

Look for medium to large artichokes, 3½ to 4 inches across (about 12 oz. *each*). Artichokes that have been cut tend to darken when exposed to air, so trim them just before cooking or place them in an acid water bath (3 tablespoons vinegar per quart of water) until you're ready to cook.

Vegetable-Ham Artichoke Salad

6 medium to large artichokes
4 quarts water
2 tablespoons vinegar
2 teaspoons salt
About 2 tablespoons lemon juice
½ cup *each* frozen peas (thawed) and diced cooked ham
1 small tomato, seeded and diced
⅓ cup *each* chopped celery and green pepper
3 tablespoons *each* chopped dill pickle and sliced green onion
Mustard dressing (directions follow)
1 hard-cooked egg, chopped

Remove coarse outer leaves from artichokes and trim stems even with base so they'll stand upright. With a sharp knife, cut off top ⅓ of each artichoke. With scissors, trim thorns from tips of remaining leaves.

In a 5-quart or larger pan, bring water, vinegar, and salt to boiling. Add artichokes; cover and boil gently until stem ends pierce readily with a fork (about 30 minutes); drain.

Let artichokes cool slightly, then pull out center leaves and scrape out fuzzy centers with a spoon. Drizzle cavities with lemon juice; cool, wrap, and refrigerate for 1 hour or until next day.

For filling, combine peas, ham, tomato, celery, pepper, pickle, and onion. Stir in ½ cup of the dressing, then mix in egg. Spoon filling into artichokes; serve remaining dressing as dipping sauce for leaves. Makes 6 servings.

Mustard dressing. Combine ½ cup **salad oil,** 3 tablespoons **lemon juice,** 3 teaspoons **Dijon mustard,** ½ teaspoon **paprika,** 1 teaspoon **garlic salt,** and dash of **pepper.** Add ¾ cup **mayonnaise** and stir to blend.

Bacon & Rice Artichoke Salad

Pictured on page 58

6 medium to large artichokes
4 quarts water
2 tablespoons vinegar
2 teaspoons salt
About 2 tablespoons lemon juice
1 small tomato, seeded and diced
8 strips bacon, fried, drained, and crumbled
1 cup cold cooked rice
⅓ cup sliced green onion
½ cup frozen peas, thawed
2 tablespoons chopped parsley
Herb-mayonnaise dressing (directions follow)

Trim, boil, prepare, and refrigerate artichokes as directed in preceding recipe.

For filling, combine tomato, bacon, rice, green onion, peas, and parsley. Stir in ½ cup of the herb-mayonnaise dressing; spoon into artichokes and serve remaining sauce for the leaves. Makes 6 servings.

Herb-mayonnaise dressing. Combine ⅓ cup **olive oil** or salad oil, 2 tablespoons **white wine vinegar,** and ¼ teaspoon *each* **dry basil, oregano leaves, garlic salt,** and **paprika.** Add 1 cup **mayonnaise** and stir to blend.

Shrimp-stuffed Artichokes

6 medium to large artichokes
4 quarts water
2 tablespoons vinegar
2 teaspoons salt
About 2 tablespoons lemon juice
½ pound small cooked shrimp
Sour cream dressing (directions follow)
Lemon wedges

Trim, boil, prepare, and refrigerate artichokes as directed in preceding recipe for vegetable-ham artichoke salad.

To serve, stir together shrimp and ½ cup of the sour cream dressing; spoon into artichokes and garnish with lemon wedges. Serve remaining dressing as sauce to dip leaves. Makes 6 servings.

Sour cream dressing. Mix together ⅔ cup **mayonnaise,** ½ cup **sour cream,** 3 tablespoons **lemon juice,** 1 teaspoon **grated lemon peel,** and ½ teaspoon *each* **salt, tarragon leaves,** and **Dijon mustard.**

...*Zarzuela (cont'd.)*

Spoon mixture into a wide, shallow serving dish. Serve with accompaniments. Makes 10 to 12 servings.

Accompaniments. Mound ½ pound **small cooked shrimp** in the center of the zarzuela. Peel and slice 1 or 2 large **avocados.** Quarter 4 to 5 **limes;** squeeze 2 or 3 limes over avocado to prevent darkening. Arrange avocado slices around shrimp; place remaining limes in a dish. Spoon 2 cups **sour cream** into a serving dish; sprinkle on a few fresh **coriander leaves** (or chopped green onion). Let guests squeeze lime and spoon sour cream over individual servings.

Fruit & Fish Rice Plate

Chilled cooked fish complemented by fruit makes a cool whole-meal salad. If you're in a hurry, substitute canned shrimp or tuna. Arrange fresh peach or apricot halves on lettuce and top with this fish-rice mixture.

- 1½ **cups cold cooked rice**
- ½ **cup** *each* **finely chopped green onion, green pepper, and celery**
- ¼ **cup** *each* **mayonnaise and sour cream**
- 1 **tablespoon lemon or lime juice**
- 2 **teaspoons curry powder**
- ¼ **teaspoon ground ginger**
  Salt and pepper
- 2 **cups (about 1 lb.) cold cooked salmon, rockfish, or lingcod (cut in chunks); or ½ pound small cooked shrimp; or 1 can (about 7 oz.) tuna, drained**
  Lettuce leaves
- 4 **large peaches or 8 large apricots, halved and pitted**

Mix together rice, onion, green pepper, and celery. Combine mayonnaise, sour cream, lemon juice, curry powder, ginger, and salt and pepper to taste; blend well. Add dressing to rice mixture; then gently mix in fish. Cover and chill for several hours.

To serve, arrange lettuce leaves on 4 individual plates, top each with 2 peach halves (peeled, if desired), and mound fish mixture evenly on top. Makes 4 servings.

CONFETTILIKE FILLING of rice, peas, diced tomatoes, and bacon bits is stuffed into whole cooked artichokes. Remaining herb-mayonnaise dressing is served as a dipping sauce for artichoke leaves. The recipe is on page 57.

Sweet & Tart Sesame-Rice Salad

Garnish individual mounds of rice-vegetable salad with a couple of chilled cooked shrimp, then sprinkle with lots of toasted sesame seed.

- 2 **cups cold cooked short grain rice (such as California pearl)**
- ½ **cup** *each* **finely chopped carrot, green onion, and cucumber**
- ¼ **cup white wine vinegar**
- 2 **tablespoons sugar**
- ½ **teaspoon salt**
- 2 **tablespoons sesame seed**
  Butter lettuce leaves
- 12 **cold cooked medium-size shrimp, shelled and deveined**

Mix together rice, carrot, onion, and cucumber. Combine vinegar, sugar, and salt; stir into rice mixture, cover, and chill for at least 1 hour or as long as overnight.

In a frying pan over medium-high heat, toast sesame seed, stirring, until golden (about 4 minutes); set aside.

To serve, line 6 salad plates with lettuce leaves. Mound equal portions of rice mixture on each plate. Garnish each salad with 2 shrimp and toasted sesame seed. Makes 6 servings.

Turkey-Rice Salad

A creamy lemon dressing enlivens this almond-topped turkey or chicken salad. Another time, try the salad with shrimp instead of turkey.

- **Lemon dressing (directions follow)**
- 3 **cups cold cooked rice**
- 3 **cups cold diced, cooked turkey or chicken, or 1 pound cooked small shrimp**
- 1 **cup** *each* **thinly sliced celery and chopped green pepper**
- 1 **can (about 8 oz.) water chestnuts, drained and sliced**
  Salt and pepper
- ½ **cup sliced almonds**

Prepare lemon dressing. Gently mix together rice, turkey, celery, green pepper, water chestnuts, and dressing until well blended. Add salt and pepper to taste. Cover and chill up to 4 hours.

Meanwhile, spread almonds in a shallow pan and toast in a 350° oven until golden (about 8 minutes). Just before serving salad, garnish with nuts. Makes about 6 servings.

Lemon dressing. In a bowl, combine ¾ cup **mayonnaise,** 1 teaspoon **grated lemon peel,** ¼ cup

lemon juice, 1 tablespoon *each* **prepared mustard** and **prepared horseradish,** and ¼ teaspoon **garlic powder;** blend well. Stir in ½ cup thinly sliced **green onion,** ¼ cup chopped **parsley,** and 1 jar (2 oz.) **pimentos** (drained and chopped).

Macaroni-stuffed Tomatoes

When cut to resemble a tulip, a tomato makes a perfect container for an individual serving of ham-and-cheese macaroni salad. You can prepare the filling up to a day ahead.

> ½ cup *each* salad macaroni, finely diced
>   cooked ham, and shredded sharp
>   Cheddar cheese
> 1 tablespoon *each* drained sweet pickle
>   relish and chopped pimento
> 2 tablespoons finely chopped onion
> ¼ cup mayonnaise
> 1 teaspoon prepared mustard
>   Salt and pepper
> 4 medium-to-large tomatoes
>   Lettuce leaves
>   Parsley sprigs

Cook macaroni according to package directions; drain well, rinse in cold water, and drain again.

Combine macaroni, ham, cheese, relish, pimento, onion, mayonnaise, and mustard; blend well and add salt and pepper to taste. Cover and refrigerate until next day, if desired.

Peel tomatoes, if desired, and cut out stems. Without cutting all the way through, cut tomatoes into 4 to 6 wedges. Arrange lettuce leaves on 4 salad plates and place 1 tomato on each. Carefully open up tomatoes like tulips and spoon equal amounts of macaroni salad into center of each.

Cover and refrigerate up to 4 hours, if desired. Garnish each with a parsley sprig. Makes 4 servings.

Shrimp & Macaroni Salad

Canned shrimp and lots of sliced egg turn macaroni salad into a cool supper entrée. Combine this colorful salad early in the day so it has a chance to chill.

> 6 ounces (about 1⅓ cups) salad macaroni
> 1 can (3½ oz.) pitted ripe olives, drained
> 1 medium-size tomato, peeled, seeded,
>   and chopped
> 1 can (4½ oz.) small cooked shrimp,
>   drained
> ¾ cup chopped sweet pickle
> ⅔ cup sliced green onion
>   Creamy dressing (directions follow)
> 7 hard-cooked eggs, sliced
>   Salt and pepper

Cook macaroni according to package directions; drain well, rinse in cold water, and drain again. Chop about ¾ of the olives.

In a large bowl, combine macaroni, chopped olives, tomato, shrimp, pickle, and ½ cup of the onion. Prepare creamy dressing, pour over macaroni mixture, and mix well. Gently stir in most of the egg slices and salt and pepper to taste; cover and refrigerate for at least 2 hours.

To serve, garnish with remaining whole olives, green onion, and egg. Makes 8 servings.

Creamy dressing. Stir together ⅔ cup *each* **sour cream** and **mayonnaise,** 2 tablespoons **sweet pickle juice,** 1 tablespoon **prepared mustard,** 1 teaspoon **sugar,** ½ teaspoon **Worcestershire,** and ⅛ teaspoon **liquid hot pepper seasoning.**

Macaroni-Egg Salad

If it's your turn to make the salad for a buffet dinner or picnic, consider this one—it easily serves 10 to 12 people. It's full of chopped dill pickle and lots of bacon.

> 1 pound salad macaroni
> 12 green onions, thinly sliced (including tops)
> 4 hard-cooked eggs, chopped
> 1 cup thinly sliced celery
> 12 slices crisply cooked bacon, crumbled
> 1 jar (4 oz.) sliced pimentos, drained
> 1 cup chopped dill pickle
> 1½ cups mayonnaise
> 1 tablespoon prepared horseradish
> 2 teaspoons prepared mustard
> 1 tablespoon dill pickle juice (optional)
>   Salt and pepper

Cook macaroni according to package directions; drain well, rinse in cold water, and drain again. Turn macaroni into a large salad bowl. Add onion (reserving some green tops for garnish), eggs, celery, bacon, pimento, and pickle.

Combine mayonnaise, horseradish, mustard, and pickle juice (if used); blend well. Stir into macaroni mixture; season to taste with salt and pepper and garnish with reserved onion tops. Cover and chill for 4 to 6 hours. Makes 10 to 12 servings.

Tuna-Noodle Salad ✓

Twisty noodles lend visual interest to this vegetable-bedecked whole-meal salad.

- 4 ounces twisty noodles
- 1 large can (12½ oz.) tuna, drained
- 1 package (10 oz.) frozen peas, thawed
- ½ cup seeded and chopped green pepper
- ½ cup *each* thinly sliced radishes, celery, mushrooms, and green onion
  Relish dressing (directions follow)
- 2 medium-size tomatoes, cut in wedges
- 3 hard-cooked eggs, sliced

Cook noodles according to package directions; drain well, rinse in cold water, and drain again. Turn noodles into a large salad bowl. Break tuna into chunks and distribute over noodles. Add peas, pepper, radishes, celery, mushrooms, and onion. Prepare dressing; spoon over salad and toss gently until well blended. Cover and chill for 4 to 6 hours.

To serve, toss well and garnish with tomatoes and eggs. Makes 6 to 8 servings.

Relish dressing. Combine ¾ cup **mayonnaise**, ½ cup **tomato-based chili sauce,** ⅓ cup **sweet pickle relish**, ½ teaspoon **prepared horseradish**, and **salt** and **pepper** to taste.

Chicken Noodle Pineapple Boats

Spoon chicken noodle salad into hollowed-out pineapple shells. Leave stem ends on pineapple for decoration. You can even assemble this curry-

- 1 small pineapple
- ¼ cup slivered almonds
- 1 package (3 oz.) Oriental chicken noodle soup mix
- 3 to 4 cups cold diced cooked chicken
- 1 can (6 oz.) water chestnuts, drained and sliced
- 1 small green pepper, seeded and chopped
- ¼ cup thinly sliced green onion
- ⅓ cup *each* mayonnaise and sour cream
- 2 tablespoons chopped Major Grey's chutney
- 2 teaspoons lemon juice
- 1½ teaspoons curry powder
- 1 teaspoon Dijon mustard
- ⅛ teaspoon cayenne
  Lettuce leaves (optional)

Cut pineapple into quarters lengthwise through crown. With a curved grapefruit knife, cut pineapple flesh from shell; remove and discard core and cut flesh into bite-size chunks; reserve. Set pineapple shells, cut side down, to drain.

Spread almonds in a shallow pan and toast in a 350° oven for about 8 minutes or until golden; set aside.

Cook Oriental noodles according to package directions. Drain well, turn into a large bowl, and toss with flavor packet contents. When cool, add pineapple chunks, chicken, water chestnuts, pepper, and onion.

Combine mayonnaise, sour cream, chutney, lemon juice, curry powder, mustard, and cayenne; blend well. Add dressing to noodle mixture and mix gently but thoroughly. Cover and chill pineapple shells for as long as 24 hours.

Before serving, stir salad mixture well. Arrange lettuce leaves on 4 individual plates, if desired. Place pineapple shells on each plate; fill each shell with an equal portion of salad mixture. Sprinkle evenly with almonds. Makes 4 servings.

Chicken Noodle Salad (recipe below)

Chicken-Noodle Salad

Egg noodles are a surprising addition to this meal-size salad. Both noodles and chicken can be cooked

- 6 ounces (about ¾ cup) medium egg noodles
- ½ cup salad oil
- ¼ cup lemon juice
- 1½ teaspoons garlic salt
- 2 teaspoons sugar
- 1 teaspoon *each* dry mustard and crumbled rosemary
- ½ teaspoon pepper
- 3 cups cold shredded cooked chicken
- ½ cup *each* chopped parsley and thinly sliced green onion
- 4 cups *each* lightly packed broken spinach and chicory leaves, or 8 cups lightly packed broken spinach leaves

(Continued on next page)

...*Chicken-Noodle Salad (cont'd.)*

Cook noodles according to package directions; drain, rinse well in cold water, and drain again.

Combine salad oil, lemon juice, garlic salt, sugar, mustard, rosemary, and pepper; blend well.

In a large bowl, mix together noodles and chicken. Add dressing and toss gently. Cover and chill for at least 1 hour or up to 4 hours.

To serve, add parsley, onion, and broken greens; toss lightly. Makes 4 to 6 servings.

Tabbuli

Pictured on facing page

Middle Eastern cracked wheat salad is highly flavored with mint and green onion. It can be made several days ahead, then assembled to serve with tomato wedges and romaine leaves.

- 1 cup bulgur wheat
- 1 cup cold water
- ½ cup *each* minced parsley and green onion
- ¼ cup *each* chopped green pepper and fresh mint (or 2 tablespoons dry mint)
- 1 large tomato, peeled and chopped
- 4 tablespoons *each* olive oil and lemon juice
  Salt
  Inner romaine leaves
  Tomato wedges

Rinse bulgur wheat several times, then combine with cold water and let stand for 1 hour; drain off any remaining liquid.

Combine bulgur wheat with parsley, onion, pepper, mint, tomato, oil, and lemon juice; toss gently to blend. Add salt to taste.

Cover and chill until serving time. Mound tabbuli in a serving bowl and surround with romaine leaves and tomato wedges. Diners can scoop up tabbuli onto romaine leaves and top with tomato wedges to eat. Makes 6 to 8 servings.

Orange-Wheat Salad

Bulgur wheat and orange sections team up in this unusually tasty salad. A citrus juice and mayonnaise dressing can be made just before serving.

- 1 cup bulgur wheat
- 2 cups water
- 1 can (11 oz.) mandarin oranges, drained
- ¼ cup mayonnaise
- 2 tablespoons *each* lemon juice and orange juice
- 2 teaspoons chopped chives
- 1 teaspoon *each* sugar and salt

In a large pan, combine wheat and water. Bring to a boil, reduce heat, cover, and simmer for 15 minutes or until liquid is absorbed. Remove lid to let steam escape so the cooked wheat will dry a bit; cool and then add orange sections (reserve a few sections for garnish). Chill until ready to serve.

Combine mayonnaise, lemon juice, orange juice, chives, sugar, and salt. Pour over chilled wheat and toss gently. Garnish with reserved orange sections. Makes 4 to 6 servings.

Cracked Wheat & Cabbage Salad

Cooked bulgur wheat gives a nutlike flavor to this crunchy vegetable slaw dotted with shredded carrot.

- ½ cup bulgur wheat
- 1 cup water
  Salt
- ½ cup mayonnaise
- 3 tablespoons cider vinegar
- 2 tablespoons sugar
- ¼ teaspoon *each* liquid hot pepper seasoning, dill weed, and Dijon mustard
- ½ cup thinly sliced green onion
- 1½ cups finely shredded cabbage
- ½ cup *each* thinly sliced celery and shredded carrot

In a 2-quart pan, combine wheat, water, and ½ teaspoon salt. Bring to boil, reduce heat, cover, and simmer for 15 minutes or until liquid is absorbed.

Meanwhile, combine mayonnaise, vinegar, sugar, hot pepper seasoning, dill weed, mustard, and onion; blend well. Add dressing to hot cooked wheat and mix thoroughly. Cover and chill well (until next day, if desired).

About 1 hour before serving, combine wheat mixture with cabbage, celery, and carrot. Season to taste with salt.

Spoon mixture into a salad bowl, cover, and chill until serving time. Makes 4 to 6 servings.

FROM MIDDLE EASTERN MARKETS and Mediterranean cooks comes tabbuli—the nut-flavored bulgur wheat salad flavored with mint, onion, olive oil, lemon, and tomatoes. The recipe is on this page.

chpt. 4   goes from pg. 64 to 73

Fruit Salads

These natural beauties need little help in showing off their glowing colors and interesting shapes. To avoid disguising delicate flavors, go lightly on dressings.

Tossed Fruit Salad

Four fruits are tossed with an oil and lemon-lime juice dressing.

  1 small grapefruit
  1 medium-size pear
  1 cup seedless grapes
  1 can (11 oz.) mandarin oranges, drained
 ¼ cup olive oil or salad oil
  1 tablespoon *each* lemon juice and lime juice
  1 teaspoon salt
 ¼ teaspoon paprika
     Dash of cayenne
     Chicory, watercress, or lettuce

Remove peel and white membrane from grapefruit; lift out sections. Also peel, core, and dice pear. In a large bowl, mix together grapefruit, pear, grapes, and oranges. Combine oil, lemon juice, lime juice, salt, paprika, and cayenne; blend well. Pour over fruit and mix lightly, then chill. Serve on a bed of greens. Makes 6 servings.

Cantaloupe & Raspberries

Raspberries are puréed with cream sherry to mix with cubed cantaloupe and whole berries for a delightful opening salad course or dessert. Serve in stemmed sherbet glasses.

    About 2 cups raspberries
  3 tablespoons sugar
 ¼ cup cream sherry
  1 large cantaloupe

Whirl enough raspberries in a blender to make ½ cup purée. (Cover and chill remaining berries.) Force purée through a wire strainer to remove seeds, if desired. Place purée in a bowl and blend in sugar and cream sherry.

Halve cantaloupe, scoop out seeds, and remove fruit. Discard shell; cut fruit into bite-size pieces. Mix cantaloupe into purée.

To serve, spoon purée mixture into sherbet glasses or bowls. Top with remaining berries. Makes 6 to 8 servings.

Fruit & Nut Summer Slaw

Add a few fruit surprises—banana, apple, oranges —to ever-popular coleslaw. Then dress it with an orange-flavored yogurt.

- 1 can (11 oz.) mandarin oranges
- 5 cups finely shredded cabbage
- 1 cup thinly sliced celery
- ½ cup raisins or chopped dates
- 1 large banana
- 1 tart apple
- 2 tablespoons lemon juice
- ½ cup chopped nuts
- 1 cup orange-flavored yogurt
- ½ teaspoon salt
- ¾ teaspoon poppy seed

Drain mandarin oranges, reserving syrup. In a serving bowl, mix together oranges, cabbage, celery, and raisins.

Slice banana and dice apple; combine with mandarin syrup and lemon juice; pour over banana and apple stirring to coat, to prevent darkening. Then, with a slotted spoon, remove fruit and add to slaw along with nuts.

Combine 2 tablespoons of the juice mixture with yogurt and salt; blend until smooth. Pour over salad and mix gently; sprinkle with poppy seed. Makes 4 to 6 servings.

Minted Melon Balls

A clear glass salad bowl will show off an assortment of melon balls from your choice of melons— red watermelon, green honeydew, and orange cantaloupe or Crenshaw. Serve with a chilled citrus syrup, flavored with fresh mint.

- ⅓ cup sugar
- ½ cup water
- 1½ tablespoons coarsely chopped fresh mint or 2 teaspoons dry mint
- 2 tablespoons orange juice
- 1 tablespoon lemon juice
- 2 quarts assorted melon balls or bite-size cubes (see suggestions above) Mint sprigs

In a small pan over high heat, combine sugar and water; bring to a boil, stirring, until sugar is dissolved; then boil for 5 minutes. Remove from heat and pour over mint; cover and chill for about 1 hour. Then pour syrup through a wire strainer and discard mint. Stir in orange juice and lemon juice; cover and chill thoroughly.

To serve, pile melon balls in a serving bowl, arranging them in layers, if desired. Pour chilled syrup over melon and garnish with mint sprigs.

Spoon into individual bowls to serve. Makes 6 to 8 servings.

Cherry Salad with Sesame Seed

Orange-flavored sesame dressing puts the finishing touch on a tossed salad of cantaloupe, pineapple, avocado, and lots of deep red cherries.

- Sesame-orange dressing (directions follow)
- 1 medium-size head iceberg lettuce
- 1 medium-size cantaloupe
- 1 medium-size avocado
- 1 small pineapple, peeled, cored, and cut in bite-size chunks or 1 can (1 lb. 13 oz.) pineapple chunks, drained
- 1½ cups pitted Bing or Royal Ann cherries
- ½ teaspoon salt
- 1½ tablespoons lemon juice

Prepare sesame-orange dressing; set aside. Line a salad bowl with outer lettuce leaves; break remaining lettuce into bite-size pieces. Halve cantaloupe, scoop out seeds, and remove fruit. Discard shell; cut fruit into bite-size pieces. Peel, pit, and cut avocado in bite-size pieces; mix with lettuce pieces, cantaloupe, avocado, pineapple, cherries, salt, and lemon juice. Pile into lettuce-lined salad bowl. Pass dressing to spoon over individual servings. Makes 6 servings.

Sesame-orange dressing. Spread 2 tablespoons **sesame seed** in a shallow pan and toast in a 350° oven for 8 minutes or until golden. Mix together 1 cup **sour cream,** 3 tablespoons *each* **lime juice** and undiluted **frozen orange juice concentrate,** ¼ teaspoon **salt,** and the toasted sesame seed.

Minted Melon Balls (recipe at left)

66/.

Gingered Tropical Fruit Plate

Pictured on facing page

Instead of a sweet dessert, why not wind up dinner with a fruit salad? Fruit can be as refreshing at the end of a meal as at the beginning. This salad is dressed with a honey-ginger topping. For a low-calorie rendition, substitute unflavored yogurt for sour cream.

  2 medium-size bananas
1½ tablespoons lemon juice
  2 oranges
  1 medium-size pineapple, peeled, and cut in ½-inch rounds
  1 papaya, peeled, seeded, and cut in ½-inch lengthwise slices
    Raspberries (optional)
    Red or green grapes (optional)
    Lime wedges (optional)
    Ginger dressing (directions follow)

Cut bananas into ½-inch diagonal slices; toss with lemon juice. Also remove peel and white membrane from oranges and cut into thin, crosswise slices. On each of 4 salad plates, place 2 or 3 slices of banana, orange, pineapple, and papaya. Garnish with raspberries, grapes, and lime wedges if you wish. Prepare ginger dressing and pass to spoon over individual servings. Makes 4 servings.

Ginger dressing. Stir together 1 cup **sour cream** or unflavored yogurt and 1½ tablespoons *each* **honey** and chopped **candied ginger;** cover and chill, if made ahead.

Coriander-spiced Crenshaw Melon

Often you can find half Crenshaw melons—just right for this salad—in the produce section of your market. Just slice the melon and serve it with this simple lime-honey dressing.

¼ cup lime juice
1½ tablespoons honey
  1 tablespoon coarsely chopped fresh coriander (cilantro) or 1 teaspoon dry cilantro leaves
½ large Crenshaw melon, peeled and sliced into thin, lengthwise crescents
    Whole coriander leaves (optional)

Stir together lime juice, honey, and 1 tablespoon chopped coriander; cover and chill for several hours.

To serve, arrange melon slices on 4 to 6 plates with slices overlapping slightly. Garnish each with coriander leaves, if desired. Pass dressing to spoon over individual servings. Makes 4 to 6 servings.

Waldorf Salad

As the name would indicate, the Waldorf Astoria Hotel in New York City auditioned this salad and brought it fame. Basically an apple-walnut combination, it goes together in minutes.

  1 large red Delicious apple
  1 cup *each* halved seedless grapes and diced celery
½ cup *each* chopped walnuts and mayonnaise

Dice the apple and mix with grapes, celery, walnuts, and mayonnaise. Chill 1 to 6 hours. Makes 4 servings.

Hot Spiced Fruit Salad

In winter when fewer fresh fruits are available, this salad is especially appreciated because it uses mostly canned fruits. They are baked in a syrup seasoned with butter and spices. Think of serving this salad with turkey or a ham—it serves a crowd.

  1 can (1 lb.) *each* peach halves, pineapple chunks, and pitted light sweet cherries
  1 can (1 lb.) *each* pear halves and apricot halves, drained
  2 tart apples
  3 tablespoons lemon juice
½ teaspoon *each* ground nutmeg and cinnamon
¼ teaspoon ground cloves
⅓ cup firmly-packed brown sugar
¼ cup butter or margarine
  3 bananas
  2 cups seedless grapes (fresh or canned)
    Sour cream, whipped cream, or unflavored yogurt (optional)

Drain and combine syrup from peaches, pineapple, cherries, pears, and apricots, reserve 1½ cups of the combined fruit syrup. Core and dice apple; mix with lemon juice. Turn all drained fruits into a 2½-quart baking dish. Stir together reserved fruit syrup, nutmeg, cinnamon, cloves, and brown sugar; pour over fruit. Dot fruit with butter. Cover and bake in a 350° oven for 20 minutes. Peel banana and cut into chunks. Lightly stir grapes and bananas into baked fruit, cover, and bake for 5 more minutes. Serve hot with sour cream, if desired. Makes 12 servings.

A REFRESHING END TO A MEAL, this individual fruit salad features thick slices of tropical fruits. Top it with ginger dressing. The recipe is on this page.

Fruit-stuffed Pineapple Shells

Let the host or hostess serve this fruit salad from the pineapple shells at the table. A mint-yogurt dressing can be passed to pour over the individual servings. Some people might like papaya seeds in the dressing; that idea is optional.

   1 **small pineapple**
   1 **large papaya**
   1 **orange**
  ¼ **cup chopped dates**
  ¾ **cup unflavored yogurt**
   1 **tablespoon honey**
   1 **tablespoon chopped fresh or
      1½ teaspoons dry mint**
   2 **bananas**
  ¼ **cup** *each* **chopped macadamia nuts and
      shredded coconut**

Cut pineapple in half lengthwise through crown. Cut out fruit from each half leaving a ½-inch-thick shell. Cut away and discard core; cut fruit into bite-size chunks. Cut papaya in half, peel, and scoop out seeds, reserving 1 tablespoon seeds for dressing, if desired. Cut pulp into bite-size pieces. Remove peel and white membrane from orange; lift out sections. In a bowl, mix together pineapple, papaya, orange, and dates. Cover and chill up to 4 hours.

Mash papaya seeds, if used, and mix with yogurt, honey, and mint; cover and chill.

To serve, slice bananas; mix with other fruit. Spoon fruit into pineapple shells, then sprinkle with macadamia nuts and coconut. Pass yogurt dressing to spoon over individual servings. Makes 6 servings.

Fruit-filled Honeydew Wedges (recipe at right)

Peanut & Tofu-filled Pineapple Boats

Used as serving containers, half pineapple shells filled with deep-fried tofu puffs and peanuts provide a high protein meal for two. Look for tofu puffs in Oriental grocery stores.

   1 **large pineapple
      Peanut sauce (directions follow)**
   1 **small cucumber, thinly sliced**
  ¼ **pound fresh bean sprouts**
   2 **tablespoons thinly sliced green onion**
  ½ **cup sliced canned water chestnuts or
      sliced celery
      About 1½ ounces Japanese-style deep-
      fried tofu puffs, cut in ¾-inch cubes,
      or 5 ounces Chinese-style tofu puffs**
  ¼ **cup coarsely chopped salted roasted
      peanuts**

Cut pineapple in half lengthwise through crown. With curved grapefruit knife, remove fruit leaving a ½-inch-thick shell. Cut away and discard core; cut enough fruit into ¾-inch cubes to make 2 cups; reserve remaining fruit for another use; drain shells. Meanwhile, prepare peanut sauce.

Just before serving, drain pineapple cubes; mix together with cucumber, bean sprouts, onion, water chestnuts, tofu, and peanut sauce. Spoon equal portions into pineapple shells and sprinkle with peanuts. Makes 2 servings.

Peanut sauce. Stir together ⅓ cup **chunk-style peanut butter,** 3 tablespoons firmly-packed **brown sugar,** ¼ to ½ teaspoon **crushed red pepper,** and ¼ cup **lemon juice.**

Fruit-filled Honeydew Wedges

A cool green wedge of sweet honeydew is served with sliced peaches and berries, topped with a tart creamy dressing, for a first-course salad or dessert.

   1 **cup sour cream**
  1½ **tablespoons honey**
  ½ **teaspoon dry mustard**
   2 **teaspoons lemon juice**
   1 **honeydew melon, cut into 6 or 8 wedges**
   4 **peaches or nectarines**
   1 **cup** *each* **blueberries and raspberries
      or strawberries**

Combine sour cream, honey, mustard, and lemon juice; blend well, cover, and chill.

Place a melon wedge on 6 to 8 individual salad plates. Peel and slice peaches; place on top of honeydew with berries. Pass chilled dressing to spoon over servings. Makes 6 to 8 servings.

Summer Salad

Crushed strawberries distinguish the dressing for this colorful fruit combination. For a low-calorie dressing variation, substitute unflavored yogurt for sour cream.

  1 basket (about 12 oz.) strawberries
  1 cup sour cream or unflavored yogurt
  1 tablespoon *each* sugar and orange juice
  1 medium-size cantaloupe
  2 or 3 cups watermelon balls
  ¾ to 1 pound seedless grapes
  2 large peaches
     About 1 tablespoon lemon juice
     Ground nutmeg
     Mint sprigs

Rinse and hull berries. Crush enough small ones to make ½ cup (reserve larger berries); combine with sour cream, sugar, and orange juice until well blended; cover and chill.

Halve cantaloupe, scoop out seeds, and remove fruit. Discard shell; cut fruit into bite-size pieces.

Mix reserved berries together with cantaloupe, watermelon balls, and grapes. Peel, pit, and thinly slice peaches; mix with lemon juice to prevent darkening, and add to other fruits. Sprinkle with nutmeg and stir gently to blend. Cover and chill for 1 to 2 hours.

Serve fruits in individual bowls. Spoon sour cream dressing evenly on top and garnish each serving with a mint sprig. Makes 6 to 8 servings.

Golden Apple Salad ✓

Golden Delicious apples are available year-round in most areas, making this salad an always-easy one to create with shredded carrots and canned pineapple.

  2 medium-size Golden Delicious apples
  2 tablespoons lemon juice
  1 can (13 oz.) pineapple tidbits
  2 medium-size carrots, shredded
  1 package (3 oz.) cream cheese
     (at room temperature)
  1½ teaspoons grated lemon peel
  2 teaspoons sugar
  ¼ teaspoon *each* ground nutmeg and salt
     Lettuce leaves
     Chopped salted peanuts

Core but do not peel apples; cut into ½-inch cubes and turn to coat in lemon juice. Drain pineapple, reserving 1 tablespoon of the syrup. Mix together apples, pineapple, and carrots.

Combine cream cheese with the reserved 1 tablespoon pineapple syrup, lemon peel, sugar, nutmeg, and salt; blend well. Gently mix into apple mixture.

To serve, line a rimmed serving plate or salad bowl with lettuce leaves. Mound apple mixture on greens and sprinkle nuts on top. Makes 4 to 6 servings.

Homemade Croutons

That partial loaf of leftover French bread needn't be tossed out. Consider making your own seasoned croutons. From about ⅓ of a 1-pound loaf of French bread you'll get about 2 cups croutons. They can be stored in a covered jar at room temperature for several weeks.

Basic Seasoned Croutons

Cut day-old **French bread** (about ⅓ of a 1-lb. loaf) into ½-inch cubes to make 2 cups total. Evenly spread cubes on a rimmed baking sheet; bake in a 300° oven for 10 minutes. Remove from oven; reset oven temperature to 275°.

In a wide frying pan or wok over medium heat, melt ¼ cup **butter** or margarine. Stir in your choice of **seasoning mixes** described below. There are three flavors to choose from: Italian herb and cheese, herb and onion, and garlic.

Add toasted bread cubes to seasoned butter and toss to coat as evenly as possible. Spread cubes out on baking sheet again and return to 275° oven. Bake for 30 minutes longer or until cubes are crisp and light brown. Cool completely and store in a covered jar. Makes about 2 cups croutons.

Italian herb & cheese. Stir into the **melted butter** ½ teaspoon **Worcestershire** and 1 teaspoon **Italian seasoning** (or ¼ teaspoon *each* oregano, thyme, marjoram leaves, and dry basil). Remove from heat and stir in 1 tablespoon grated **Parmesan cheese.**

Herb & onion. Stir into the **melted butter** 1 teaspoon **onion powder,** ½ teaspoon *each* **dry basil, chervil,** and **oregano leaves.** Remove from heat.

Garlic. Stir into the **melted butter** 1 large clove **garlic** (minced or pressed) and 1 teaspoon **parsley flakes.** Remove from heat.

Fruit Tray with Honey-Lemon Dressing

Pictured on facing page

Displayed in rows on a serving platter, there's nothing more beautiful than fruit on a table. It can pass as a centerpiece until dinner or serve as a buffet entrée for self service. The cream cheese dressing is spooned over servings. If you prefer more tartness, add more lemon juice.

- 1 large cantaloupe, peeled, seeded, and cut lengthwise in ½-inch-wide slices
- 3 kiwi, peeled, and thinly sliced
- 1 small pineapple, peeled, cored, and cut in short spears
- ¼ small watermelon, cut in 1½-inch-wide slices
- 1 small orange, peeled (if desired) and sliced
  Red grapes
- ½ small honeydew melon, cut in wedges (optional)
  Creamy honey-lemon dressing (directions follow)

On a large serving platter, arrange in rows: cantaloupe, kiwi, pineapple, watermelon, orange, grapes, and honeydew, if you wish. Prepare honey-lemon dressing and pass to spoon over individual servings. Makes 6 servings.

Creamy honey-lemon dressing. In a blender, whirl 1 small package (3 oz.) **cream cheese** until smooth. Add 2 tablespoons **honey**, 3 tablespoons **lemon juice**, ½ teaspoon **grated lemon peel**; whirl to blend. With motor on slow speed, gradually add ¾ cup **salad oil** in a slow steady stream. Add **cayenne** and **salt** to taste; chill until serving time.

Apple & Zucchini Salad

Prepare this crispy red and green vegetable-fruit combination early in the day so flavors have a chance to mingle.

- ⅓ cup salad oil
- 1 tablespoon lemon juice
- 2 tablespoons white wine vinegar
- 1 teaspoon *each* sugar and dry basil
  Salt
- ¼ teaspoon pepper
- 3 medium-size red apples
- ½ medium-size red onion, thinly sliced lengthwise
- 1 green pepper, seeded and cut in matchstick-size pieces
- 1 pound zucchini, thinly sliced

In a serving bowl, combine oil, lemon juice, vinegar, sugar, basil, ¾ teaspoon salt, and pepper; blend well. Core and dice apple; add to dressing, turning to coat. Distribute onion, green pepper, and zucchini over apple. Mix together gently but thoroughly, then cover and chill for several hours.

To serve, mix salad again and add more salt to taste, if desired. Makes about 6 servings.

Quick Avocado-Grapefruit Salad

Bottled Italian dressing is the short-cut for this salad-in-a-hurry to serve on plates alongside a main dish.

- 2 medium-size grapefruit
- 2 medium-size avocados
  Butter lettuce leaves
  Bottled Italian-style oil and vinegar dressing

Remove peel and white membrane from grapefruit; lift out sections. Peel, pit, and slice avocado. On 6 salad plates, arrange slices of avocado and grapefruit sections on butter lettuce leaves. Pass Italian dressing to pour over individual servings. Makes 6 servings.

Citrus-Spinach Salad

Orange and grapefruit sections, combined with green spinach leaves, make a very pretty dinner salad capped with sliced mushrooms and crisp bacon.

- 2 or 3 large oranges
- 2 large grapefruit
- 1 large bunch spinach (about 1¼ lbs.), torn into bite-size pieces
- 1 can (8 oz.) water chestnuts, drained and thinly sliced
- ¼ pound mushrooms, thinly sliced
- 6 strips crisply cooked bacon, crumbled
  Soy dressing (directions follow)

Remove peel and white membrane from oranges and grapefruit; lift out sections from each. Place spinach in a large bowl; sprinkle over the oranges and grapefruit sections, water chestnuts, mushrooms, and bacon.

Prepare soy dressing and pour over salad; toss lightly. Makes 6 to 8 servings.

Soy dressing. Combine ⅓ cup **salad oil**, 3 tablespoons **white wine vinegar**, 1 tablespoon **soy**

HANDSOME PLATTERFUL OF ASSORTED FRUITS in overlapping rows can be featured as a beautiful centerpiece on a dinner table or buffet. The recipe is on this page.

sauce, 2 teaspoons **sugar,** ½ teaspoon **salt,** and ⅛ to ¼ teaspoon **liquid hot pepper seasoning;** blend well.

Pineapple-stuffed Avocado

Pineapple chunks and banana slices, mixed with a creamy mint dressing, are spooned into the centers of avocado halves.

> ¼ cup *each* **mayonnaise and sour cream**
> 3 tablespoons finely chopped **fresh mint** or 2 tablespoons **dry mint**
> 2 teaspoons **sugar**
> ¼ teaspoon **liquid hot pepper seasoning**
> 2 tablespoons **lemon juice**
> 3 large **avocados**
> 2 small **bananas**
> ½ cup chopped **celery**
> 1 cup fresh or canned **pineapple chunks,** drained
> **Mint sprigs**

Combine mayonnaise, sour cream, mint, sugar, hot pepper seasoning, and ½ tablespoon of the lemon juice; blend well, cover, and chill.

Cut avocados in half lengthwise and remove pit; sprinkle evenly with remaining 1½ tablespoons lemon juice to prevent discoloration. Thinly slice bananas and mix with celery and pineapple chunks. Add chilled dressing and toss to coat.

To serve, spoon mixture evenly into avocado centers. Garnish with mint sprigs. Makes 6 servings.

Gazpacho-stuffed Avocado

Cold and colorful gazpacho mixture fills the centers of avocado halves. The salad ingredients are the same as for a popular Spanish cold soup.

> 3 medium-size **avocados**
> 3 tablespoons **lemon juice**
> 1½ cups peeled, seeded, and chopped **tomato**
> ½ cup diced peeled **cucumber**
> ¼ cup *each* chopped **green pepper** and **green onion**
> 1 small clove **garlic,** minced or pressed
> 1 tablespoon **red wine vinegar**
> 2 tablespoons **olive oil** or **salad oil**
> ½ teaspoon **salt**
> ⅛ teaspoon **liquid hot pepper seasoning**
> 3 cups shredded **iceberg lettuce**
> **Sour cream**

Cut avocados in half lengthwise and remove pits. Spoon out pulp in large pieces, leaving about ¼-inch thickness of avocado in skin. Brush all exposed surfaces of avocado in shells with about 1 tablespoon of the lemon juice; cover and chill. Dice avocado pulp and combine with remaining lemon juice, tomato, cucumber, pepper, onion, garlic, vinegar, olive oil, salt, and hot pepper seasoning. Mix lightly, then cover and chill for several hours.

Divide lettuce evenly among 6 salad plates. Place an avocado shell on each plate. Mound equal amounts of gazpacho mixture into each shell. Pass sour cream to spoon over individual servings. Makes 6 servings.

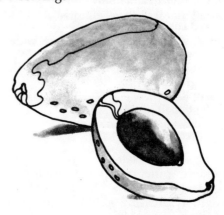

Hawaiian Salad with Curry Dressing

Macadamia nuts sprinkled over Hawaiian fruits make an appetizing presentation for a summer meal. Everything is embellished with a lime and ginger-curried dressing.

> 2 medium-size or large **avocados**
> 3 or 4 **bananas**
> About 2 tablespoons **lemon** or **lime juice**
> 2 large **oranges**
> 1 medium-size **pineapple,** peeled, cored, and cut into pieces
> 2 tablespoons chopped **candied ginger**
> **Lime-curry dressing** (directions follow)
> ½ cup coarsely chopped **macadamia nuts**
> **Thin lime slices**

Peel, pit, and cut avocados into chunks. Cut bananas in 1-inch-thick diagonal slices. Mix avocado and bananas with lemon juice. Remove peel and white membrane from oranges; add sections with pineapple to avocado mixture. Sprinkle with ginger and cover and chill, if made ahead.

Prepare lime-curry dressing. Toss fruit gently to mix, sprinkle with macadamias, and garnish with thin lime slices. Serve with lime-curry dressing to spoon onto individual portions. Makes 8 to 10 servings.

Lime-curry dressing. Blend together ⅓ cup **lime juice,** ½ cup **salad oil,** 2 tablespoons **rum,** 1 tablespoon **sugar,** ½ teaspoon **curry powder,** and 1 tablespoon finely minced **crystallized ginger;** do not refrigerate.

Fresh Orange & Onion Ring Salad

Orange and onion rings marinate in an oil-vinegar dressing before they are served, decoratively overlapping each other, on a lettuce-lined platter.

    4 large oranges
    1 large red onion, thinly sliced and
          separated into rings
    ½ cup salad oil
    ¼ cup white wine vinegar
    2 tablespoons sugar
    ¾ teaspoon paprika
    ½ teaspoon *each* salt and dry mustard
       Butter lettuce

Remove peel and white membrane from oranges; cut into thin crosswise slices. Layer oranges and onion in a shallow bowl. Combine oil, vinegar, sugar, paprika, salt, and mustard; blend well. Pour over oranges and onion, tossing to coat. Cover and chill for at least 2 hours or until next day.

To serve, arrange lettuce leaves on serving platter. Lift oranges and onion rings from dressing and arrange on lettuce. Pass marinade to spoon over servings. Makes 6 to 8 servings.

Gold & Crimson Salad

Crumbled dry mint flavors the creamy dressing for this beet and fruit salad. Chill the beets and pineapple separately, then drain well before serving. Substitute unflavored yogurt for sour cream in the dressing, if you are counting calories.

    1 can (about 13 oz.) pineapple chunks or
          tidbits, drained
    1 can (about 8 oz.) water chestnuts, drained
          and sliced
    ¼ cup salad oil
    1 teaspoon sugar
    3 tablespoons lemon juice
    ¼ teaspoon paprika
    3 tablespoons minced onion
       Salt and pepper
       Creamy dressing (directions follow)
    1 can (1 lb.) sliced pickled beets, chilled
          and drained
       Lettuce leaves

Combine pineapple and water chestnuts in a bowl. In a small jar, combine oil, sugar, lemon juice, paprika, onion, and salt and pepper to taste. Shake well, then pour over pineapple mixture. Cover, and refrigerate for at least 4 hours or until next day. Prepare and chill creamy dressing.

To serve, arrange beets on a lettuce-lined platter. Drain pineapple and water chestnuts (discard marinade) and mound onto beets. Pass creamy dressing to pour over individual servings. Makes 6 servings.

Creamy dressing. Combine 1 cup **sour cream** or unflavored yogurt, 1 tablespoon finely chopped **green onion,** 1 teaspoon **dry mint,** and **salt** and **pepper** to taste; blend well and chill.

Mexican Cucumber & Orange Salad Tray

Despite its simplicity, a tray salad can be strikingly handsome, with the contrasting colors and textures of the foods emphasized by the orderly arrangement. You can assemble this fruit and vegetable combination well ahead, cover it tightly with clear plastic wrap, and chill until time to serve.

    2 medium-size cucumbers
    ⅓ cup white wine vinegar
    ½ cup olive oil or salad oil
    ½ teaspoon salt
    4 large oranges
    1 large avocado
       About 1 tablespoon lemon juice
    1 large mild onion (red or white), cut in
          thin, vertical slices
       Butter lettuce
       Orange-chili dressing (directions follow)

With a vegetable peeler, peel lengthwise strips from each cucumber skin, leaving cucumbers with alternating patterns of green and white. Thinly slice cucumbers and place in a bowl. Add vinegar, oil, and salt; mix, cover, and chill for at least 1 hour.

Remove peel and white membrane from oranges; cut into crosswise slices. Peel, pit, and slice avocado; coat with lemon juice. Drain cucumbers and reserve marinade. On a large rimmed tray, arrange in rows, cucumbers, oranges, avocado, and onions. Garnish tray with lettuce. If made ahead, cover with clear plastic wrap and chill up to 3 hours. Prepare orange-chili dressing. To serve, spoon dressing onto individual portions. Makes 8 to 10 servings.

Orange-chili dressing. Combine reserved cucumber marinade with 1½ teaspoons **grated orange peel,** ½ teaspoon **chili powder,** and ¼ teaspoon **salt;** blend well. (Do not refrigerate.)

chpt. 5 - *grp fm p 74 to 85...*

Molded Salads

Creamy or sparkling clear, brimming with fruits or vegetables
or both, molded salads add a festive note.

Thinly Sliced Ham in Aspic

Here is a simplified version of the French classic,
jambon en persil. Paper-thin slices of cooked ham
in aspic are punctuated with parsley and green
onion and served with a mustard sauce.

- 2 **envelopes unflavored gelatin**
- ½ **cup cold water**
- 2 **cans (14 oz.** *each***) regular-strength chicken broth**
- 2 **chicken bouillon cubes or 2 teaspoons chicken stock concentrate**
- 2 **tablespoons white wine vinegar**
- ¼ **teaspoon liquid hot pepper seasoning**
- ½ **cup** *each* **thinly sliced green onion and lightly packed minced parsley**
- ¾ **pound very thinly sliced cooked ham**
  Mustard sauce (directions follow)

Sprinkle gelatin over cold water; let stand for 5
minutes to soften. In a pan, combine chicken broth,

bouillon cubes, vinegar, and hot pepper seasoning;
bring to boiling. Add softened gelatin, stirring
until completely dissolved; remove from heat.

Chill gelatin until thick and syrupy. Gently stir
in green onion and parsley; pour mixture into a
6-cup ring mold. Using a spoon, lightly push individual slices of ham down into gelatin to create a
rippled effect. Cover and chill until firm (at least 4
hours).

Prepare mustard sauce. Unmold salad on a serving platter and serve with mustard sauce to spoon
over individual servings. Makes about 6 servings.

Mustard sauce. Mix together 1 cup **mayonnaise,**
½ cup **sour cream,** 3 tablespoons **prepared mustard,** and 2 teaspoons **sugar.**

*INDIVIDUAL MOLDS of cranberry-raspberry
gelatin make an attractive addition to a
turkey-time dinner. The recipe for
Two-berry Salad is on page 82.*

Guacamole Salad Ring (recipe on page 77)

Avocado-Lime Mousse with Chutney Chicken Salad

A chutney chicken salad is piled into the center of this white wine and avocado creation. Serve it when you really want to impress guests with your imagination.

Chutney dressing (directions follow)
1 package (3 oz.) lime-flavored gelatin
½ cup boiling water
½ cup dry white wine
1 package (3 oz.) cream cheese, at room temperature
2 medium-size avocados
⅓ cup mayonnaise
1 tablespoon lime juice
2 tablespoons thinly sliced green onion
½ cup finely diced celery
½ teaspoon salt
Lettuce leaves
Cherry tomato halves

Prepare chutney dressing and chill for several hours or until next day, if desired.

Dissolve gelatin in boiling water; stir in wine and set aside. Beat cream cheese in a bowl until smooth. Peel, pit and mash avocados; stir into cream cheese with the mayonnaise, lime juice, onion, celery, salt, and gelatin mixture. Pour into a 1-quart ring mold, cover, and chill until firm (at least 3 hours).

Unmold jelled salad ring on a serving platter and garnish with lettuce and tomato halves; pile chicken salad in center of ring. Makes 4 servings.

Chutney dressing. Stir together ½ cup **mayonnaise**, 2 teaspoons **lime juice**, ¼ teaspoon **salt**, ¼ cup finely chopped **Major Grey's chutney**, and 1 teaspoon **curry powder.** Pour dressing over 3

cups diced **cooked chicken** and mix well. Cover and chill for several hours or until next day.

Chicken in Aspic

From Sweden comes chicken in aspic, served with a piquant mustard dressing and lavishly garnished with crisp and juicy vegetables. Offer a dark bread and butter plus some pickled beets. For heartier appetites, you might add small, boiled new potatoes accented with a dill-flavored butter.

1 large broiler-fryer chicken (about 3½ lbs.), cut in pieces
2¾ cups water
½ cup white wine
4 chicken bouillon cubes or 4 teaspoons chicken stock concentrate
5 whole black peppers
2 bay leaves
1 large onion, quartered
2 small carrots, sliced
4 to 5 sprigs parsley
¼ cup thinly sliced green onion
2 envelopes unflavored gelatin
Salt and pepper
Mustard dressing (directions follow)
Watercress, sliced cucumbers, cherry tomato halves (optional)

Place chicken in a 5-quart pan with 2½ cups of the water. Add wine, bouillon cubes, pepper, bay, onion, carrot, and parsley. Cover and simmer until chicken is fork-tender (about 40 minutes).

Lift out chicken and set aside. Pour broth through wire strainer into a bowl; discard vegetables, then chill broth. Meanwhile, remove skin and bones from chicken; cut meat into ½-inch cubes and combine with green onion in 1½ to 2-quart mold. Cover and chill.

Lift off and discard solidified fat from chilled broth, place broth in a pan, and boil, uncovered, until reduced to 3 cups. Meanwhile, sprinkle gelatin over remaining ¼ cup water; let stand for 5 minutes to soften, then stir into hot broth until dissolved. Add salt and pepper to taste, then pour over chicken and onion in mold. Cover and chill until firm (at least 6 hours).

Prepare mustard dressing. Unmold salad on a serving platter; garnish with watercress, cucumber, and tomatoes. Pass dressing to spoon over individual servings. Makes 4 to 6 servings.

Mustard dressing. Combine ½ cup *each* **mayonnaise** and **sour cream**, 2 teaspoons **Dijon mustard**, 1 teaspoon **lemon juice**, ½ teaspoon **dry rosemary**, and 1 tablespoon chopped **parsley**; add **garlic salt** and **pepper** to taste; blend well.

Ham-Swiss Cheese Salad

Diced ham and cheese make a high-protein gelatin salad for brunch or dinner. For an attractive presentation, surround mold with sliced cucumbers just before serving.

- 2 envelopes unflavored gelatin
- 1½ cups tomato juice
- 1 tablespoon wine vinegar
- ¼ teaspoon paprika
- 1 tablespoon minced onion
- 1 teaspoon Dijon mustard
- ½ cup mayonnaise
- 2 tablespoons sweet pickle relish
- 2 cups finely diced ham
- ½ cup *each* finely diced Swiss cheese and celery
  Sliced cucumbers (optional)

Sprinkle gelatin over tomato juice in a pan; let stand for 5 minutes to soften. Place over medium heat and stir until gelatin is completely dissolved. Remove from heat and stir in vinegar, paprika, onion, and mustard until well blended. Cool to room temperature.

Stir mayonnaise and pickle relish into cooled gelatin until blended. Then stir in ham, cheese, and celery. Pour into a 1-quart salad mold, cover, and chill until firm (at least 4 hours).

Unmold onto a serving platter and surround with sliced cucumbers, if you wish. Makes 4 servings.

Guacamole Salad Ring

If you make this guacamole in a ring mold, consider filling the center with shrimp, crab, or chicken for a whole-meal salad.

- 1 package (3 oz.) lemon-flavored gelatin
- 1 cup boiling water
- 2 tablespoons tomato-based chili sauce
- ¼ teaspoon liquid hot pepper seasoning
- 2 medium-size avocados
- ¼ cup *each* lemon juice and finely chopped green onion
- ½ cup thinly sliced celery
  Citrus French dressing (directions follow)
  Lettuce leaves

Dissolve gelatin in boiling water. Stir in chili sauce and hot pepper seasoning; chill until thick and syrupy. Peel, pit, and mash avocados. Blend with lemon juice. Add avocado mixture, onion, and celery to slightly thickened gelatin and stir until well blended. Pour into a 4-cup ring mold. Cover and chill until firm (at least 3 hours).

Prepare citrus French salad dressing. Unmold

salad on a serving platter; garnish with lettuce leaves and serve with citrus French dressing. Makes about 6 servings.

Citrus French dressing. Combine ¼ cup **olive oil** or salad oil, 2 tablespoons *each* **lemon juice** and **orange juice**, ½ teaspoon **dry mustard**, ¼ teaspoon **salt**, and 1 teaspoon **paprika**; blend well.

Creamy Avocado Mold

This creamy green salad can take any shape you want. One suggestion would be to chill it in a ring mold and, when ready to serve, fill the center with seafood or chicken salad.

- 1 envelope unflavored gelatin
  Water
- 2 medium-size avocados
- ¼ teaspoon grated lemon peel
- 3 tablespoons lemon juice
- ½ cup sour cream
- 2 tablespoons chopped green onion
- ½ teaspoon *each* garlic salt, salt, and liquid hot pepper seasoning
  Lettuce leaves
  Cherry tomatoes, sliced jicama, and ripe olives (optional)

In a pan, combine gelatin and ¼ cup cold water; let stand for 5 minutes to soften. Stir in 1½ cups water, place over medium heat, and stir until gelatin is dissolved; let cool.

Peel, pit, and mash avocados; mix with lemon peel, juice, sour cream, onion, garlic salt, salt, and hot pepper seasoning. Stir in cooled gelatin mixture until well blended and pour into a 1-quart mold. Cover and chill until firm (at least 3 hours).

Unmold onto a serving plate. Garnish with lettuce leaves, and cherry tomatoes, jicama, and olives, as desired. Makes 4 to 6 servings.

How to Unmold Gelatin Salads

There's really no trick to unmolding a gelatin salad. Just before serving, dip the mold up to its rim in hot tap water for 5 to 7 seconds. With a towel, quickly wipe water from the mold. Cover the mold with a plate larger than the mold and, holding plate and mold together, quickly invert. Gently shake the mold, if necessary, to loosen the salad. Remove the mold and refrigerate salad until serving time.

Molded Ham & Potato Salad

Unlike a traditional potato salad, this one uses creamy potato soup and forms the base of a hearty mold.

>   1 envelope unflavored gelatin
> 1/4 cup cold water
>   1 can (10¼ oz.) frozen cream of potato soup, thawed
> 1/4 cup milk
>   2 cups finely diced cooked ham
>   1 cup thinly sliced celery
>   1 jar (2 oz.) sliced pimento, well drained
> 1/3 cup chopped dill pickle
>   3 tablespoons sliced green onion
>   1 teaspoon *each* Dijon mustard and lemon juice
>   1 cup sour cream

In a pan, sprinkle gelatin over cold water; let stand for 5 minutes to soften. Stir in undiluted soup and milk. Place over low heat and stir occasionally until gelatin is dissolved. Remove from heat and fold in ham, celery, pimento, pickle, onion, mustard, lemon juice, and sour cream. Turn into a 1-quart mold, cover, and chill until firm (at least 3 hours). Unmold onto a serving platter. Makes 4 to 6 servings.

Dilled Shrimp Mold

Pictured on facing page

Made in a fish-shaped mold, this creamy dilled shrimp salad would also be good scooped onto crackers like a pâté.

> 3/4 cup canned tomato juice
>   1 envelope unflavored gelatin
>   1 tablespoon lemon juice
> 1/2 teaspoon salt
> 1/4 teaspoon Worcestershire
>   1 cup sour cream
> 1/4 to 1/2 teaspoon dill weed
>   About 6 ounces small cooked shrimp
>   Watercress
>   Pitted ripe olives
>   Lemon wedges

Pour tomato juice into a 2-quart pan; sprinkle in gelatin and let stand about 5 minutes. Place over medium heat and stir until gelatin is completely dissolved. Remove from heat and let cool slightly.

To gelatin add lemon juice, salt, Worcestershire, sour cream, dill, and all but 10 shrimp. Place half the mixture in a blender and whirl until smooth.

SHAPED LIKE A FISH, this creamy-smooth mold combines the subtle tastes of shrimp and dill. Garnish with whole ripe olives and lemon wedges. The recipe is on this page.

Pour into a 2½-cup mold. Whirl remaining mixture in blender until smooth and add to mold. Cover and chill for 4 hours or until set.

To serve, unmold onto a serving plate. Garnish with watercress, reserved shrimp, olives, and lemon wedges. Makes 5 to 6 servings.

Sole Mousse with Shrimp

A food processor comes in handy when puréeing fish to the creamy smooth texture desired for a mousse; however, a food grinder or blender will do nicely. Decorate sole mousse with tiny shrimp and thinly sliced cucumber. Consider serving it when entertaining a large group.

>   2 cups dry white wine
>   1 *each* onion and carrot, thinly sliced
>   2 parsley sprigs
>   1 teaspoon salt
>   8 to 10 whole black peppers
> 2½ pounds boneless sole fillets
>   2 envelopes unflavored gelatin
>   1 small onion, minced
>   3 tablespoons butter or margarine
>   2 tablespoons all-purpose flour
> 1½ cups half-and-half (light cream)
>   3 tablespoons lemon juice
>   2 teaspoons prepared mustard
>   Salt
>   2 cups whipping cream, whipped
>   1 pound small cooked shrimp
>   1 cucumber, thinly sliced

In a wide frying pan, combine wine, onion, carrot, parsley, salt, and peppers. Cover and bring to a boil; reduce heat and simmer for about 5 minutes. Place half the fish at a time in simmering broth, and cook, covered, for 2 to 3 minutes or until fish flakes readily when prodded in thickest portion with a fork.

Lift fish out of pan with a slotted spoon. Strain stock into a measuring cup and add enough cold water to make 2 cups; cool. Whirl fish in a food processor or blender until smooth, adding enough stock to make a smooth paste. Pour ½ cup of the stock into a small bowl, sprinkle gelatin over, and let stand for 5 minutes to soften.

Meanwhile, in a frying pan over medium-high heat, cook onion in butter until limp. Stir in flour and heat until bubbly; then blend in half-and-half. Cook, stirring, until thickened. Remove from heat and stir in gelatin mixture until dissolved. Add fish, lemon juice, remaining stock, mustard, and salt to taste. Chill until thick and syrupy; then fold in whipped cream. Pour into a 3-quart mold. Cover and chill until firm (at least 5 hours).

Unmold on a platter and decorate with shrimp and cucumber slices. Makes 12 to 14 servings.

Gazpacho Aspic

Finely chopped garden vegetables lace this chile-seasoned tomato gelatin. Offer it with roasted or grilled meats.

- 1 envelope unflavored gelatin
- 1 bottle (10 oz.) tomato-based chili sauce
- 2 medium-size tomatoes, peeled, seeded, and finely chopped
- 1½ cups peeled, finely chopped cucumber
- ½ medium-size green pepper, seeded and chopped
- ½ cup chopped green onion
- 1 clove garlic, minced or pressed
- 2 tablespoons olive oil or salad oil
- ¼ cup red wine vinegar
  Mexican seasoning or chili powder
  Lettuce leaves

In a small pan, sprinkle gelatin over chili sauce; let stand for 5 minutes to soften. Place over medium heat and stir until gelatin is dissolved. Let cool to room temperature.

Into cooled gelatin mixture, stir tomatoes, cucumber, pepper, onion, garlic, oil, and vinegar. Blend in Mexican seasoning to taste. Pour into a 1-quart mold or 4 to 6 individual molds. Cover and chill until firm (at least 3 hours).

Unmold on a serving plate and garnish with lettuce leaves. Makes 4 to 6 servings.

Shrimp & Artichokes in Aspic

The marinade from canned marinated artichokes adds its ready flavor to aspic filled with shrimp and artichokes.

- 3 envelopes unflavored gelatin
- 4 cups vegetable juice cocktail
- 2 tablespoons *each* lemon juice and prepared horseradish
- 1 tablespoon grated onion
- 1 teaspoon seasoned salt
- ⅛ teaspoon liquid hot pepper seasoning
  Dash of pepper
- 1 jar (6 oz.) marinated artichoke hearts
- 1 pound medium-size shrimp, cooked, shelled, deveined, and coarsely chopped
  Lettuce leaves
  Sour cream or unflavored yogurt (optional)

Sprinkle gelatin over 1 cup of the vegetable juice cocktail in a small bowl; let stand for 5 minutes to soften. Pour remaining 3 cups vegetable juice into a pan and bring to a boil; stir in gelatin mixture until completely dissolved. Remove from heat and blend in lemon juice, horseradish, onion, salt, hot

pepper seasoning, and pepper. Drain artichokes, stirring marinade into gelatin mixture. Chill gelatin mixture until thick and syrupy. Blend shrimp and artichokes into gelatin mixture; spoon into a 6½-cup ring mold. Cover and chill until firm (at least 3 hours).

Unmold on a lettuce-lined serving plate and serve with sour cream to spoon over individual servings, if you wish. Makes 6 servings.

Molded Crab Cocktail

To serve this salad as a main dish, garnish each portion with half an avocado, thinly sliced.

- 2 envelopes unflavored gelatin
  Water
- ¾ cup tomato-based chili sauce
- ⅔ cup dry white wine or chicken broth
- ½ cup sour cream or unflavored yogurt
- 1 tablespoon instant minced onion
- ½ teaspoon dill weed
- ¾ teaspoon salt
- 1 tablespoon lemon juice
- 4 hard-cooked eggs
- 1½ cups cooked or canned drained crab
- 1 can (2¼ oz.) sliced ripe olives, drained
  Lettuce leaves
  Sour cream, mayonnaise, or unflavored yogurt (optional)

Sprinkle gelatin over ½ cup water and let stand for 5 minutes to soften. In a pan, heat chili sauce and ¾ cup water. Add gelatin mixture and stir until dissolved. Remove from heat and stir in wine, sour cream, onion, dill, salt, and lemon juice. Chill until thick and syrupy.

Chop two of the eggs; stir into gelatin mixture with the crab and all but a few olive slices. Turn mixture into a 6-cup mold, cover, and chill until firm (at least 3 hours).

To serve, unmold on a serving platter; surround with lettuce leaves and garnish with reserved egg and olive slices. Pass sour cream to spoon over individual servings, if you wish. Makes 6 servings.

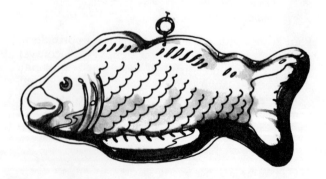

Easy Seafood Mold

Using canned seafood makes this an easy salad to prepare. It's hearty enough for a dinner salad when served with French sourdough bread and a hot soup.

   1 package (3 oz.) lemon-flavored gelatin
   1 cup boiling water
   1 can (8 oz.) tomato sauce
  ½ cup thinly sliced celery
  ¾ cup chopped or flaked cooked or canned
      drained seafood (fish, crab, or shrimp)
     Lettuce leaves
     Mayonnaise and paprika

In a bowl, dissolve gelatin in boiling water. Add tomato sauce, and stir well. Chill until mixture is thick and syrupy; then fold in celery and seafood. Pour into a shallow 8-inch square pan; cover and chill until firm (at least 3 hours).

Cut into squares and serve on lettuce leaves. Garnish with a dollop of mayonnaise and sprinkle with paprika. Makes 6 servings.

Antipasto Tuna Mold

In the Italian spirit, here's an antipasto tuna mold with a well-seasoned herb dressing. Serve it for lunch or supper with crusty bread sticks, sliced tomatoes, and dill pickles.

   2 envelopes unflavored gelatin
 2¼ cups cold water
   3 chicken bouillon cubes or 3 teaspoons
      chicken stock concentrate
   1 cup boiling water
  ⅓ cup white wine vinegar
  ½ teaspoon liquid hot pepper seasoning
  ½ cup *each* diced green pepper and sliced
      ripe olives
   1 jar (2 oz.) diced pimentos, drained
   1 can (8 oz.) garbanzos, drained
   1 can (7 oz.) tuna, drained and broken into
      chunks
     Creamy herb dressing (directions follow)
     Lettuce leaves
     Hard-cooked eggs (quartered) and
      marinated artichoke hearts
      (optional)

Sprinkle gelatin over ¼ cup of the cold water and let stand for 5 minutes to soften. Dissolve bouillon cubes in boiling water, then add gelatin and stir until dissolved. Mix in remaining 2 cups cold water, the vinegar, and hot pepper seasoning. Chill mixture until thick and syrupy.

Gently stir pepper, olives, pimentos, garbanzos, and tuna into gelatin mixture. Spoon mixture into a 1½ to 2-quart ring mold. Cover and chill until firm (about 6 hours).

Prepare creamy herb dressing. Unmold salad on a serving platter; surround with lettuce leaves and garnish with eggs and artichokes, if used. Pass dressing to spoon over individual servings. Makes 4 to 6 servings.

Creamy herb dressing. Stir together 2 tablespoons **salad oil,** 1 tablespoon **white wine vinegar,** and ¼ teaspoon *each* **dry basil** and **oregano leaves.** Mix in 1 cup **mayonnaise** until smooth; season to taste with **garlic salt.**

Broccoli & Egg Aspic

An attractive pattern of egg slices and broccoli flowerets decorates the top of this molded salad. The first layer of gelatin will set the broccoli and egg in a pattern. For a meal, serve the aspic with crusty rolls and thinly sliced ham.

     About 1 pound broccoli
     Boiling salted water
   1 envelope unflavored gelatin
  ½ cup cold water
   1 can (10½ oz.) condensed beef consommé
   1 tablespoon lemon juice
   6 hard-cooked eggs
   1 tablespoon bottled Italian salad dressing
      or salad oil
  ⅓ cup *each* mayonnaise and thinly sliced
      green onion
   2 tablespoons Dijon mustard
     Salt

Remove and discard broccoli stem ends. Wash spears well. Immerse in boiling salted water and cook, uncovered, just until tender when pierced (about 7 minutes); drain and cool.

Sprinkle gelatin over cold water in small pan; let stand for 5 minutes to soften. Place over low heat and stir until dissolved. Remove from heat and stir in consommé and lemon juice; cool to room temperature.

Thinly slice 1 of the hard-cooked eggs; reserve others. Coat bottom and sides of an 8-inch square pan with salad dressing. On bottom of pan, arrange 4 to 6 egg slices and 4 to 6 broccoli flowerets in a decorative pattern. Pour ¾ cup of the gelatin mixture over pan bottom; chill until gelatin is firm. Chill remaining gelatin separately until syrupy and slightly thickened.

Meanwhile, chop remaining eggs and broccoli and place in a bowl. Add mayonnaise, onion, and mustard; blend well. Stir in thickened gelatin and add salt to taste until well blended; pour over gelatin in pan, cover, and chill until firm (at least 3 hours). Unmold and cut in rectangles. Makes 6 servings.

Pimento-stuffed Olive Mold *(cnt)*

Sliced pimento-stuffed olives are scattered through this sparkling, transparent tomato aspic.

- 2 cans (about 1 lb. *each*) stewed tomatoes
- 2 envelopes unflavored gelatin
- 2 tablespoons sugar
- 4 tablespoons lemon juice
- About 6 drops liquid hot pepper seasoning
- 1 jar (2 or 3 oz.) pimento-stuffed green olives
- Water
- ¼ cup sliced green onion
- 1 cup thinly sliced celery
- Watercress sprigs

Turn tomatoes into a pan; break them into small pieces with a spoon. Sprinkle gelatin over top of tomatoes and let stand for about 5 minutes to soften. Stir in sugar, lemon juice, and hot pepper seasoning. Place over low heat and stir until gelatin is dissolved.

Drain liquid from olives into a measuring cup and add enough water, if needed, to make ⅔ cup. Slice olives and stir into gelatin with the liquid, onion, and celery. Turn into a 1½ to 2-quart mold. Cover and chill until firm (about 5 hours). Unmold on a serving platter and garnish with watercress sprigs. Makes 8 servings.

Layered Fruit in Wine Mold

Pictured on facing page

Glistening layers of strawberries, apricots, and grapes are set individually into slightly thickened gelatin flavored with white wine. Making the salad takes a little patience, but what a satisfying presentation when it's finished!

- 3 envelopes unflavored gelatin
- 1 bottle (24 oz.) white grape juice
- ⅓ cup sugar
- 2 cups Riesling or Gewurztztraminer wine
- 3 tablespoons *each* lemon juice and orange-flavored liqueur
- About 2 cups strawberries
- Mint leaves (optional)
- 1 can (1 lb.) apricot halves, drained
- About ½ cup seedless grapes

In a pan, sprinkle gelatin over grape juice; let stand for 5 minutes to soften. Add sugar; place over low heat and stir until gelatin and sugar dissolve.

Meanwhile, in a large bowl mix together wine, lemon juice, and liqueur; stir in gelatin mixture. Spoon ½ inch gelatin into a 2-quart glass bowl (cover remaining gelatin and let stand at room temperature).

Arrange about 1 cup of the strawberries in a ring around bowl; garnish with mint, if desired, in this and succeeding layers. Refrigerate until set. When set, spoon ½ inch gelatin mixture over berries and add a ring of apricots. Refrigerate until gelled.

Repeat process with a layer of grapes and another layer of strawberries, using up all the gelatin. Cover and chill until firmly set. Makes about 8 servings.

Two-berry Salad

Pictured on page 75

Pretty little molded salads add their decorative touch to a serving plate. They go well with turkey, pork, or beef. Double the recipe if you have more than six guests.

- 1 package (3 oz.) raspberry-flavored gelatin
- 1½ cups boiling water
- 1 can (8 oz.) whole-berry cranberry sauce
- ½ cup sour cream
- ¼ cup chopped walnuts
- ¼ teaspoon grated orange peel
- Watercress sprigs

Dissolve gelatin in boiling water, then chill until thick and syrupy. With a wire whip, stir in cranberry sauce, then mix in sour cream, nuts, and orange peel. Evenly spoon mixture into 6 individual molds (½-cup size) or a 3 to 4-cup mold. Cover and chill until firm (at least 3 hours).

Unmold on a serving platter and garnish with watercress. Makes 6 servings.

Cranberry-Pineapple Salad Mold

For a new Thanksgiving treat, substitute cranberry-pineapple mold for traditional cranberry sauce. It makes enough for a crowd.

- 1 can (about 8 oz.) crushed pineapple
- Water
- 2 packages (3 oz. *each*) lemon-flavored gelatin
- ½ cup sugar
- 1 cup finely chopped celery
- 1 pound raw cranberries, ground or very finely chopped
- ½ cup finely chopped walnuts, almonds, or pecans
- Mayonnaise or unflavored yogurt
- Lettuce leaves

(Continued on page 84)

LAYERS OF FRUIT hang suspended in sparkling-clear gelatin spiked with dry white wine and orange liqueur. The recipe is on this page.

Drain pineapple, reserving liquid. Add enough water to liquid to make 3 cups. Place in a pan and heat to boiling. Pour over lemon gelatin, add sugar, and stir until thoroughly dissolved; chill until thick and syrupy.

Fold pineapple, celery, cranberries, and nuts into thickened gelatin mixture. Pour into a 2-quart shallow pan, cover, and chill until firm (at least 2 hours).

Cut in squares, garnish with dollops of mayonnaise, and serve on lettuce leaves. Makes 12 servings.

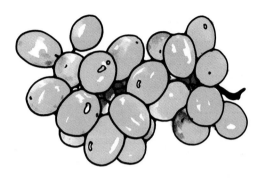

Yogurt-Fruit Salad

Lemon juice and yogurt give a fresh taste to this colorful fruit salad. Canned fruits make it a salad for any season.

    1 can (about 13 oz.) pineapple chunks
    1 can (11 oz.) mandarin oranges
    1 can (1 lb. 1 oz.) sliced peaches
      Water
    1 envelope unflavored gelatin
    1 package (3 oz.) orange-flavored gelatin
    ½ teaspoon grated lemon peel
    2 tablespoons lemon juice
      Dash of salt
    2 cups unflavored yogurt
      Lettuce leaves

Drain liquid from pineapple, mandarins, and peaches into a measuring cup; set fruits aside. Add enough water to liquid, if needed, to make 2 cups. Pour into a pan, stir in unflavored gelatin and let stand for 5 minutes to soften. Place pan over medium heat, add orange-flavored gelatin, and bring to simmering, stirring until gelatin is dissolved. Remove from heat; stir in lemon peel, juice, and salt. Cool to room temperature. With a wire whip, blend yogurt into gelatin mixture. Chill until thick and syrupy; fold in drained fruits and pour into a 2-quart mold. Cover and chill until firm (at least 3 hours).

Unmold on a serving plate and garnish with lettuce. Makes 8 servings.

Boysenberry-Nut Salad

Boysenberries and nuts add color and texture to this festive fruit salad mold. Serve honey-cream dressing in a small bowl to spoon over servings. For calorie counters, substitute unflavored yogurt for sour cream in the dressing.

    1 package (10 oz.) frozen sweetened
        boysenberries or raspberries
      Water
    1 package (3 oz.) lemon-flavored gelatin
    ¼ cup dry sherry
    1 small can (about 5 oz.) evaporated milk
    ½ cup chopped walnuts
      Honey-cream dressing (directions follow)
      Mint sprigs (optional)

Thaw berries in a strainer; reserve any liquid that drains off. Add enough water to liquid to make 1 cup. In a pan, heat liquid to boiling; remove from heat and add lemon gelatin, stirring until dissolved. Stir in sherry, then chill mixture until thick and syrupy.

Meanwhile, pour milk into a shallow bowl and set in freezer until ice crystals form around edges. Beat until soft peaks form; fold in the thickened gelatin mixture, boysenberries, and nuts. Turn into a 1-quart mold or 8 individual molds (½-cup size). Cover and chill until firmly set (at least 3 hours).

Prepare and chill honey-cream dressing.

To serve, unmold salad onto serving plate, garnish with mint sprigs, and serve with honey-cream dressing to spoon over. Makes 6 to 8 servings.

Honey-cream dressing. Mix together 1 cup **sour cream** or unflavored yogurt, and 2 teaspoons *each* **honey** and **lemon juice** until well blended. Chill until serving time.

Molded Ginger Ale & Pear Salad

Ginger ale lends its tang to a lemon-lime fruit salad. Use canned pears if fresh pears are out of season.

    1 package (3 oz.) lime-flavored gelatin
    ½ cup boiling water
    1½ cups ginger ale
    4 large fresh pears or 8 canned pear halves
        (drained)
      About 1½ tablespoons lemon juice
      Lettuce leaves
      Mayonnaise or unflavored yogurt

Dissolve gelatin in boiling water; stir in ginger ale. Chill until thick and syrupy.

Meanwhile, peel, halve, and core pears. Immediately brush surface of pears with lemon juice. Arrange pears round-side-down in a 1½-quart mold. Pour thickened gelatin over pear halves. Cover and chill until firm (at least 3 hours).

Unmold on serving platter; surround with lettuce leaves and garnish with dollops of mayonnaise. Makes 8 servings.

Strawberry Cream Layered Salad

When cut into serving pieces this salad shows off its pretty three layers. Frozen strawberries and canned pineapple make it a perfect salad for year-round use.

    1 package (3 oz.) strawberry-flavored gelatin
    ½ cup boiling water
    2 medium-size bananas
    1 package (10 oz.) frozen sweetened
        strawberries, thawed
    1 can (8 oz.) crushed pineapple, well drained
    1 cup coarsely chopped walnuts
    1 cup sour cream
        Lettuce leaves

Dissolve gelatin in boiling water. Mash bananas and combine with thawed strawberries and their juice, pineapple, and nuts. Add gelatin mixture. Pour half the mixture into an 8-inch square baking dish; cover and chill until firm (about 1½ hours). Cover remaining gelatin mixture and let stand at room temperature. When refrigerated portion is firm, spread evenly with sour cream. Spoon remaining gelatin mixture evenly over cream layer. Cover and chill until firm (at least 4 hours). Arrange lettuce on 6 salad plates. Cut salad into squares and place on lettuce. Makes 6 servings.

Buttermilk Fruit Ring

Salads are a summer cook's best friend because they can fit into menus in a variety of ways. This cool molded salad is low in calories and can serve as a pretty dessert as well.

    1 envelope unflavored gelatin
    1 cup *each* buttermilk and orange juice
    3 tablespoons honey
        About ½ small cantaloupe
    2 medium-size peaches
    1 cup sliced strawberries
    ½ cup chopped walnuts

In blender jar, sprinkle gelatin over buttermilk; let stand for 5 minutes to soften. Heat orange juice to boiling, then add to blender along with honey.

Cover and whirl on low speed until well blended. Pour mixture into bowl, cover, and chill until thick and syrupy.

Halve cantaloupe, scoop out seeds, and remove fruit. Discard shell; cut fruit into small pieces (you should have about 1½ cups). Peel and slice peaches; stir berries, cantaloupe, walnuts, and peaches into gelatin mixture and pour into a 1-quart ring mold. Cover and chill until firm (about 4 hours).

Unmold on a serving plate. Makes 4 to 6 servings.

Yogurt Curried Salad

The spices and creamy smooth texture of this curry-flavored salad disguise the fact that its calories are few. You can serve it with a variety of meat, poultry, or fish main dishes.

    2 tablespoons butter or margarine
    ¼ cup finely chopped onion
    2 teaspoons curry powder
    ½ cup firmly-packed brown sugar
    2 envelopes unflavored gelatin
    ½ teaspoon ground ginger
    2 teaspoons chicken-flavored stock base
    6 tablespoons white or cider vinegar
    1 cup water
    1 large container (32 oz.) unflavored yogurt
        Lettuce leaves (optional)

In a frying pan, melt butter over medium heat. Add onion and curry powder; cook, stirring, until onion is limp.

In a bowl, combine sugar, gelatin, ginger, and stock base. Stir in vinegar and water; let stand for 5 minutes to soften gelatin. Add gelatin mixture to onion-curry mixture and heat, stirring, until gelatin is thoroughly dissolved; remove from heat. With wire whip, beat in yogurt until smoothly blended. Turn into a 1½-quart salad mold, cover, and chill until firm (at least 3 hours).

Unmold salad onto a serving plate. Garnish with lettuce leaves, if you wish. Makes 8 servings.

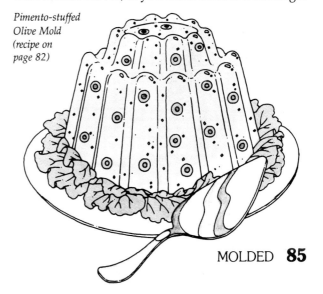

Pimento-stuffed Olive Mold (recipe on page 82)

Salad Dressings

Perfect flavor balance is an achievement born of bringing salad ingredients together with just the right dressing—and it's in this chapter that you'll find that dressing.

Sweet & Spicy French Dressing

Try this tangy French dressing with spinach, romaine, watercress, or cooked vegetables.

- ½ cup sugar
- 1 tablespoon all-purpose flour
- ½ cup cider vinegar
- 1 teaspoon *each* salt and Worcestershire
- ½ cup finely chopped onion
- 1 clove garlic, minced or pressed
- 1 cup salad oil
- ⅓ cup catsup
- 1 teaspoon celery seed

In a small pan, combine sugar, flour, and vinegar. Cook, stirring, over medium heat until bubbly and thickened; pour into blender container. Add salt, Worcestershire, onion, and garlic; whirl until smooth. With blender set on lowest speed, gradually add oil in a slow steady stream until blended. Transfer mixture to a bowl and stir in catsup and celery seed. If made ahead, cover and refrigerate. Store for as long as 4 weeks. Makes about 2 cups.

All-purpose Vinaigrette Dressing

This classic French oil and vinegar dressing is flavored with Dijon mustard and shallots. You can use it on any green salad.

- 1 tablespoon finely chopped shallots or or red onion
- 1 tablespoon Dijon mustard
- 3 tablespoons wine vinegar
- ½ cup olive oil or salad oil

In a container, combine shallots, mustard, vinegar, and oil; blend well. If made ahead, cover and refrigerate. Store for as long as 2 weeks. Makes about ¾ cup.

CLASSIC INGREDIENTS for zesty blue cheese dressing include sour cream, Worcestershire, liquid hot pepper seasoning, garlic, lemon juice, and crumbled Roquefort or other blue-veined cheese. The recipe is on page 89.

Lemon-Thyme Dressing

This refreshing dressing for green salads uses lemon juice instead of vinegar to mingle with thyme and lots of minced parsley.

- ½ cup salad oil
- 1½ teaspoons grated lemon peel
- ¼ cup lemon juice
- 1 small clove garlic, minced or pressed
- 1¼ teaspoons sugar
- ¾ teaspoon thyme leaves
- ½ teaspoon salt
- ⅛ teaspoon pepper
- ⅓ cup finely chopped parsley

In a container, combine oil, lemon peel, juice, garlic, sugar, thyme, salt, and pepper; blend well. Just before serving, stir in parsley. If made ahead, cover and refrigerate. Store for as long as 1 week. Makes about 1 cup.

Mustard-Tarragon Dressing

The addition of hard-cooked eggs to this oil-vinegar-mustard mixture turns it into a thick and creamy dressing. Serve it with greens or a chef-style salad.

- 1 cup salad oil
- ½ cup tarragon wine vinegar
- ¼ cup Dijon mustard
- 1 teaspoon *each* salt and tarragon leaves
- 2 small cloves garlic, minced or pressed
- 2 hard-cooked eggs, cut in pieces

In a blender, combine oil, vinegar, mustard, salt, tarragon, garlic, and eggs; whirl until smooth. If made ahead, cover and refrigerate. Store for as long as 1 week. Makes 2 cups.

Toasted Sesame Seed Dressing

Nutlike sesame seed dressing can be made with sour cream, or you can use sour half-and-half for fewer calories. It is great for mixed green salads.

- 2 tablespoons sesame seed
- ¼ cup olive oil or salad oil
- 1 tablespoon *each* lemon juice and honey
- 1 teaspoon curry powder
- 1 cup sour cream or sour half-and-half
- Salt and pepper

Spread sesame seed in a frying pan and cook over medium heat, stirring, until golden (3 to 5 minutes); let cool.

In a container, stir together oil, lemon juice, honey, toasted sesame seed, curry, sour cream, and salt and pepper to taste. Cover and refrigerate for at least 1 hour to allow flavors to blend. If made ahead, store for as long as 5 days. Makes about 1½ cups.

Homemade Mayonnaise

Pictured on page 91

Freshly made mayonnaise can be whipped up in a blender or food processor, and you can add to the basic recipe in many ways for flavor variations. Chutney mayonnaise is nice with fruit salad, curry mayonnaise with artichokes or seafood salad. Try green mayonnaise with seafood salad and horseradish mayonnaise with vegetable or seafood salad. Russian mayonnaise goes well with green, vegetable, egg, or seafood salad; anchovy mayonnaise with vegetable, green, or seafood salad.

Whole-egg mayonnaise is softer than mayonnaise made with egg yolks alone. But egg yolks not only make a thicker, stiffer sauce, they also add a richer flavor.

- 1 large whole egg or 3 egg yolks
- 1 teaspoon Dijon mustard
- 3 teaspoons wine vinegar or lemon juice
- 1 cup salad oil

In a blender or food processor fitted with a metal or plastic blade, place egg, mustard, and vinegar. Whirl until well blended (about 4 seconds). With motor running on slowest speed, add oil—just a few drops at a time at first, then increasing to a slow, steady stream about 1/16 inch wide. (The secret is to add oil as slowly as possible.)

If made ahead, cover and refrigerate. Store for as long as 2 weeks. Makes 1½ cups.

Chutney mayonnaise. Follow previous directions for **homemade mayonnaise,** but add 2 to 4 tablespoons **prepared chutney** to blender; whirl until smooth (about 2 minutes).

Curry mayonnaise. Follow previous directions for **homemade mayonnaise,** but reduce **Dijon mustard** to ½ teaspoon and add 1 teaspoon **curry powder** to blender; whirl until smooth.

Green mayonnaise. Place 8 sprigs **watercress,** 6 to 10 **spinach leaves,** 5 sprigs **parsley** in a bowl; cover with **boiling water** and let stand for about 5 minutes. Drain, rinse in cold water, and drain again. Follow previous directions for **homemade mayonnaise,** but add 2 teaspoons **lemon juice** to blender; whirl until smooth.

Horseradish mayonnaise. Follow previous directions for making **homemade mayonnaise,** but add

2 tablespoons **prepared horseradish** to blender; whirl until smooth.

Russian mayonnaise. Follow previous directions for **homemade mayonnaise,** but add 2 tablespoons **chili sauce,** 2 tablespoons finely chopped **pimento** or green pepper, ½ teaspoon **vinegar,** and ½ teaspoon **paprika** to blender; whirl until smooth. Stir in 1 **hard-cooked egg** and 1 tablespoon chopped **chives,** if desired:

Anchovy mayonnaise. Follow previous directions for **homemade mayonnaise,** but add 6 **anchovy fillets** or 2 tablespoons anchovy paste to blender; whirl for about 2 minutes or until blended.

Thousand Island Dressing

Creamy, pink, and probably the most familiar of the salad dressings, thousand island dressing is best served on very crisp greens, such as iceberg lettuce.

- 2 cups mayonnaise, homemade (page 88) or purchased
- ½ cup tomato-based chili sauce
- 1 tablespoon minced onion
- 2 tablespoons *each* minced green pepper and pimento
- ¼ cup sweet pickle relish
- 2 hard-cooked eggs, finely chopped
  Salt and pepper
  Half-and-half (light cream—optional)

In a bowl, combine mayonnaise, chili sauce, onion, green pepper, pimento, pickle relish, eggs, and salt and pepper to taste; blend well. Thin with a little half-and-half, if desired. If made ahead, cover and refrigerate. Store for as long as 1 week.

Low-cal Thousand Island-style Dressing

Buttermilk helps trim calories from the original thousand island dressing; but to lower them even further, use imitation mayonnaise in this dressing.

- ½ cup tomato-based chili sauce
- 1 tablespoon instant minced onion
- 2 tablespoons chopped dill pickle
- ½ teaspoon *each* grated lemon peel and prepared horseradish
- ½ cup mayonnaise, homemade (page 88) or purchased (regular or imitation)
- 1 hard-cooked egg, chopped
- 4 to 6 tablespoons buttermilk
  Garlic salt, pepper, and liquid hot pepper seasoning

In a bowl, combine chili sauce, onion, pickle, lemon peel, horseradish, mayonnaise, and egg; blend well. Stir in buttermilk until dressing is as thin as you like. Season to taste with garlic salt, pepper, and hot pepper seasoning. If made ahead, cover and refrigerate. Store for as long as 1 week. Makes 1 cup.

Creamy Louis Dressing

Try this Louis dressing on such whole-meal salads as tuna, crab, shrimp, or chicken; on wedges of iceberg lettuce; or on a cabbage slaw.

- 1 cup mayonnaise, homemade (page 88) or purchased
- ⅓ cup tomato-based chili sauce
- ¼ cup sweet pickle relish
- 3 tablespoons finely chopped green pepper
- ⅛ teaspoon liquid hot pepper seasoning
- ½ cup whipping cream

In a bowl, combine mayonnaise, chili sauce, relish, green pepper, and hot pepper seasoning; blend well. Beat cream until soft peaks form; fold into mayonnaise mixture. If made ahead, cover and refrigerate. Store for as long as 5 days. Stir gently before serving. Makes about 2 cups.

Creamy Blue Cheese Dressing

Pictured on page 86

Officially, when a dressing is called Roquefort, it must be made from real French Roquefort cheese. Since Roquefort has a sharper flavor than other blue-veined cheeses, you might want to use a little less of it in your dressing.

- 1 pint sour cream or sour half-and-half
- 1 tablespoon lemon juice
- ½ teaspoon Worcestershire
- ⅛ teaspoon liquid hot pepper seasoning
- 1 clove garlic, minced or pressed
- 8 ounces blue-veined cheese or 6 ounces Roquefort, crumbled
  Pepper

(Continued on next page)

...*Creamy Blue Cheese Dressing (cont'd.)*

In a bowl, combine sour cream, lemon juice, Worcestershire, hot pepper seasoning, and garlic; blend well. Stir in blue cheese, mashing any large pieces with a fork, until well blended. Add pepper to taste. If made ahead, cover and refrigerate. Store for as long as 10 days. Makes about 2½ cups.

Herbed Buttermilk Dressing

By varying the seasonings a bit, you can concoct your own favorite flavored buttermilk salad dressing. To lower the calories even more, substitute imitation mayonnaise for the real thing.

   1   **cup buttermilk**
   2   **tablespoons** *each* **chopped parsley and minced onion**
   ¼   **teaspoon** *each* **dry basil, oregano leaves, dry rosemary, and savory leaves**
   1   **clove garlic, minced or pressed**
   1   **cup mayonnaise, homemade (page 88) or purchased (regular or imitation)**
       Salt and pepper
   8   **ounces blue-veined cheese, crumbled (optional)**

In a bowl, combine buttermilk, parsley, onion, basil, oregano, rosemary, savory, and garlic; let stand for 5 minutes. Beat in mayonnaise and season to taste with salt and pepper. If made ahead, cover and refrigerate. Store for as long as 1 week.

Before serving, gently stir in cheese, if you wish. Makes about 2 cups.

Green Goddess Dressing

This dressing was created by Palace Hotel chefs in San Francisco during the mid-20s.

   1   **clove garlic, minced or pressed**
   ¼   **cup** *each* **coarsely chopped parsley, green onion, and watercress**
   ½   **teaspoon salt**
   1   **teaspoon tarragon leaves**
   1   **teaspoon anchovy paste or finely chopped anchovy fillets**
   2   **teaspoons lemon juice**
   1   **cup mayonnaise, homemade (page 88) or purchased**

In a blender, place garlic, parsley, onion, watercress, salt, tarragon, anchovy paste, lemon juice, and mayonnaise; whirl until smooth. If made ahead, cover and refrigerate. Store for as long as 1 week. Makes about 1½ cups.

Low-cal Green Goddess Yogurt Dressing

Like the traditional green goddess dressing, this low-calorie version complements any lettuce or seafood salad.

   1   **teaspoon tarragon leaves**
   2   **tablespoons tarragon wine vinegar**
   1   **green onion, thinly sliced**
   1½ **tablespoons minced parsley**
   2   **teaspoons anchovy paste or finely chopped anchovy fillets**
   2   **teaspoons sugar**
   ½   **teaspoon salt**
   1   **cup unflavored yogurt**

Place tarragon and vinegar in a blender; let stand for 5 minutes. Add onion, parsley, anchovy paste, sugar, salt, and yogurt; whirl until smooth. If made ahead, cover and refrigerate. Store for as long as 1 week. Makes about 1¼ cups.

Old-fashioned Boiled Dressing

Many cooks still maintain that boiled dressing makes the best coleslaw or potato salad. You may want to thin the dressing with fruit juice or milk or fluff it up with whipped cream.

   1   **tablespoon all-purpose flour**
   1   **tablespoon sugar**
   1   **teaspoon** *each* **dry mustard and salt**
       Dash of cayenne
   2   **eggs, well beaten**
   ¾   **cup milk**
   ⅓   **to ½ cup vinegar, heated**
   1   **tablespoon butter or margarine**
       Fruit juice, milk, or whipped cream (optional)

In top of double boiler, stir together flour, sugar, mustard, salt, cayenne, eggs, and milk; stir in heated vinegar. Place over boiling water and cook, stirring, until thickened (about 10 minutes). Remove from heat and add butter, stirring until smooth. If made ahead, cover and refrigerate. Store for as long as 1 week.

If you prefer a thinner dressing, stir in several tablespoons fruit juice or milk. If you prefer a thicker dressing, fold in whipped cream. Makes about 1⅓ cups.

THE SECRET OF MAKING MAYONNAISE—
whether in a food processor or a blender—is
to add the oil as slowly as possible. Recipes for
homemade mayonnaise are on page 88.

Avocado Dressing

Tangy avocado dressing will keep its color for as long as 5 days if stored airtight in the refrigerator. Thick and green, it is wonderful spooned over wedges of iceberg lettuce.

    1   large avocado
    2   tablespoons lime or lemon juice
    1½   teaspoons garlic salt
    ¼   teaspoon ground cumin
    ⅓   cup regular-strength beef broth
    1   can (4 oz.) diced green chiles

Peel, pit, and slice avocado and place in a blender; add lime juice, garlic salt, cumin, and beef broth; whirl until smooth. Transfer mixture to a bowl; stir in chiles. Cover and chill, if made ahead. Makes about 1 cup.

Creamy Tomato Dressing

Make this slightly sweet dressing several hours ahead, then serve it over any green salad.

    1   can (10½ oz.) condensed tomato soup
    ¾   cup red wine vinegar
    1   cup salad oil
    ½   cup sugar
    ½   teaspoon white pepper
    2   teaspoons salt
    1   teaspoon *each* dry mustard, prepared
         horseradish, and paprika
    1   clove garlic, minced or pressed

In a blender, combine tomato soup, vinegar, oil, sugar, pepper, salt, mustard, horseradish, paprika, and garlic; whirl at low speed until smooth. If made ahead, cover and refrigerate. Store for as long as 2 weeks. Makes about 3 cups.

Poppy Seed Dressing

This sweet-tart honey dressing is good with fruit salads as well as green salads. It is perhaps best known for its pairing with grapefruit sections and avocado slices.

    ¼   cup honey
    ½   teaspoon salt
    1   teaspoon *each* dry mustard, paprika,
         and grated lemon peel
    6   tablespoons lemon juice
    1   cup salad oil
    1 to 2 tablespoons poppy seed

In a blender, combine honey, salt, mustard, paprika, lemon peel, and lemon juice; whirl until blended.

With blender set on lowest speed, slowly add salad oil in a thin stream until blended. Transfer mixture to a bowl and stir in poppy seed. If made ahead, cover and refrigerate. Store for as long as 1 week. Makes about 1½ cups.

Creamy Onion Dressing

Here's another smooth-tart dressing for vegetable salads.

    1   cup coarsely chopped green onion
    ½   cup mayonnaise, homemade (page 88)
         or purchased
    2   large cloves garlic, minced or pressed
    2½   tablespoons white wine vinegar
    1½   teaspoons *each* salt and dry mustard
    ¼   teaspoon white pepper
    1½   cups sour cream or sour half-and-half

In a blender, combine onion, mayonnaise, garlic, vinegar, salt, mustard, and pepper; whirl until smooth. Transfer mixture to a bowl and stir in sour cream. If made ahead, cover and refrigerate. Store for as long as 5 days. Makes 2 cups.

Yogurt & Honey-Mint Dressing

Fruit salads, or vegetable salads such as green pea, benefit from this sweet-tart dressing. Made with low-fat yogurt, it is particularly shy of calories.

    ½   cup unflavored yogurt
    1   tablespoon honey
    2   teaspoons finely chopped fresh mint, or
         1 teaspoon dry mint
    1   teaspoon lemon juice

In a container, stir together yogurt, honey, mint, and lemon juice. Cover and chill for at least 1 hour to allow flavors to blend. If made ahead, store for as long as 5 days. Makes about ½ cup.

Home-flavored Vinegar

Pictured on page 94

Fresh garden herbs and whole spices are ideal ingredients for flavoring vinegars. Whether you grow your own herbs, buy them from your market, or get them in pots from the nursery, making flavored vinegar is an extremely simple process. You need to allow several weeks for the vinegar to stand and absorb the herbs' flavors; the effect is a softening and mellowing of the vinegar's sharp flavor, resulting in delightful blends. In addition to the ones we give here, try fresh dill, varieties of thyme, or shallots.

The basic method is to put the herb or herbs of your choice into a clean jar or decorative bottle, fill it with cider or wine vinegar, put on the lid or cap, and allow the herbs to flavor the vinegar. If you want to speed up the process so you can start enjoying the vinegar in a week or two, first heat the vinegar to lukewarm (or even boiling), then pour it into bottles over crushed or coarsely chopped herb leaves. Let the bottles stand in a warm, dark place and shake gently each day. When the flavor suits you, strain out the seasonings and discard, then return the vinegar to the bottle.

To make clear vinegars that have whole herbs intact, you must allow more time for the flavoring process. Do not crush the herb leaves or heat the vinegar at all, and let bottles stand in a cool, dark place without shaking them. It takes about 3 to 4 weeks for flavor to develop.

Finally, identify the vinegar's flavor by writing it on a tag or decorative label. You may want to indicate the date of bottling, too.

Once vinegars have been opened, store them in a cool, dark place and use within 3 or 4 months.

Grape & Rosemary Vinegar

Wash and dry 1 leafy sprig (about 5 inches long) *each* rosemary and lemon thyme (optional). Place herbs in pint bottle with 4 whole black peppers and 5 small fresh or canned grapes; fill bottle with white wine vinegar.

Sweet Basil & Oregano Vinegar (or Tarragon Vinegar)

Wash and dry 1 leafy sprig (about 5 inches long) *each* sweet basil and oregano (or use 2 sprigs fresh tarragon). Place herbs in a pint bottle with 4 whole black peppers and fill with red wine vinegar.

Lemon-Mint Vinegar

With a small sharp knife, cut from 1 lemon a continuous spiral strip of peel about ¼ inch wide. Wash and dry 2 leafy sprigs of mint. Place mint, lemon rind, and 6 dried currants in pint bottle and fill with white wine vinegar.

Garlic & Green Onion Vinegar

Peel 1 or 2 cloves garlic and 1 green onion (about 6 inches long). Place in a pint bottle and fill with white wine vinegar.

Orange Custard Dressing

This boiled dressing is delightful for fruit salads. For a low-calorie alternative, try the lemon-yogurt variation that follows the basic recipe.

- ½ **cup sugar**
- 1 **tablespoon cornstarch**
- ¼ **teaspoon salt**
- ⅔ **cup orange juice**
- ⅓ **cup lemon juice**
- 1 **teaspoon grated orange peel**
- 2 **eggs**
- ½ **cup whipping cream (whipped) or**
     1 cup whipped dessert topping

In a pan, blend sugar, cornstarch, and salt. Stir in orange juice, lemon juice, and orange peel. Cook, uncovered, over medium heat, stirring, until mixture boils and thickens.

In a small bowl, lightly beat eggs. Stir some of the hot sauce into eggs, then stir all into mixture in pan; heat, stirring, for 1 minute. Remove from heat and cool for 10 minutes, stirring occasionally. Cover and refrigerate for at least 2 hours. If made ahead, store for as long as 5 days.

Just before serving, fold in whipped cream. Makes about 2 cups.

Lemon-yogurt dressing. Follow recipe for orange custard dressing, but substitute **water** for orange juice, **grated lemon peel** for orange peel, and 1 cup **unflavored yogurt** for whipping cream. Makes about 2 cups.

Index

BOTTLED VINEGARS include (left to right) Grape & Rosemary, Sweet Basil & Oregano, Parsley-Black Pepper, Lemon-Mint, Garlic & Green Onion, and Oregano. Recipes are on page 93.

A Handy Metric Conversion Table

To change	To	Multiply by
ounces (oz.)	grams (g)	28
pounds (lbs.)	kilograms (kg)	0.45
teaspoons	milliliters (ml)	5
tablespoons	milliliters (ml)	15
fluid ounces (fl.oz.)	milliliters (ml)	30
cups	liters (l)	0.24
pints (pt.)	liters (l)	0.47
quarts (qt.)	liters (l)	0.95
gallons (gal.)	liters (l)	3.8
inches	centimeters (cm)	2.5
Fahrenheit temperature (°F)	*Celsius temperature (°C)*	*5/9 after subtracting 32*